MW00353552

bright SPOTS

Motivation and Inspiration to Light Your Path in a Changing World

COMPILED BY
CATHY L. DAVIS

BRIGHT SPOTS
Motivation and Inspiration to Light Your Path in a Changing World
UpsiDaisy Press

Published by **UpsiDaisy Press**, St. Louis, MO
Copyright ©2020 Cathy L. Davis
All rights reserved.

No part of this publication may be reproduced, stored in a retrieval system, or transmitted in any form or by any means, electronic, mechanical, photocopying, recording, scanning, or otherwise, except as permitted under Section 107 or 108 of the 1976 United States Copyright Act, without the prior written permission of the Publisher. Requests to the Publisher for permission should be addressed to Office@daviscreative.com, please put **Bright Spots** in the subject line.

Limit of Liability/Disclaimer of Warranty: While the publisher and author have used their best efforts in preparing this book, they make no representations or warranties with respect to the accuracy or completeness of the contents of this book and specifically disclaim any implied warranties of merchantability or fitness for a particular purpose. No warranty may be created or extended by sales representatives or written sales materials. The advice and strategies contained herein may not be suitable for your situation. You should consult with a professional where appropriate. Neither the publisher nor author shall be liable for any loss of profit or any other commercial damages, including but not limited to special, incidental, consequential, or other damages.

All contributing authors to this anthology have submitted their chapters to an editing process, and have accepted the recommendations of the editors at their own discretion. All authors have approved their chapters prior to publication.

Cover and Interior Design: Davis Creative, DavisCreative.com
Writing Coach and Editor: Kay Uhles, KayClarkUhles.com

Compilation by Cathy Davis
Bright Spots: Motivation and Inspiration to Light Your Path in a Changing World

ISBN: 978-0-9774886-9-8 (paperback)
       978-1-7347971-2-1 (ebook)

2020

To all the Light Workers,
Beacons of Light, and Living Lighthouses…

Be the spark in someone's life.

Especially when life appears to be so dark.

DEAR WORLD

I want you to stop.
I want you to be still.
I want you to rest.

I want you to open your eyes and see the gift you have been given.
The gift of time.
I want you to use this gift of time very wisely, not to create, or to achieve…
But to be still.
To be present. To be here now.
This is a time in your life, a one and only period, to *not* achieve anything.
This is a time to *not* push yourself.
This is a time to *not* be busy.
This is a time to *not* feel inadequate.

I pressed pause so that you may look around
and see everyone else in the same position.
So that you would not feel guilt, pressure, or competition.
Whilst you do this, the planet heals, the people heal,
and a collective consciousness raises its vibration and evolves.

To those of my children who have not been given rest during this time,
You honour me with your courage and your dedication.
I am proud of you all.
Come together my little ones.

Come together in spirit, by staying apart.
Be still.

— Mother Nature.

Donna Ashworth
Author, *History Will Remember When the World Stopped…*
ladiespassiton.com/
www.facebook.com/ladiespassiton

Table of Contents

The Power is in the Pause

"...in a dark night, the eye begins to see"

— e.e. cummings

For many people, the year 2020 has evolved into a process of transformation, much like that as described in Joseph Campbell's *The Hero's Journey*. A familiar storyline used by many throughout history in literature, theatre, and on the movie screen, Campbell frames the initial stage of the hero's journey process as the "call" to adventure…

Stage 1: Departure

As our own hero, we depart from the world we know (our comfort zone) and encounter the unknown with a sense of powerlessness. We feel unstable, unsure of ourselves, and under pressure to re-stabilize our world.

Stage 2: Initiation

This is *The Pause* stage—where we learn more about ourselves as we encounter time to review, rethink, and reimagine. We may feel unsafe as we face a series of trials and tribulations, yet we somehow find a way to keep going.

Stage 3: Transformation

As we endure the trials and hardships of the adventure, we undergo a personal transformation. We begin to regain a sense of balance as we learn to step into our own power. We return "home" with a better understanding of our "self" and the world.

We are ALL in *The Pause*.

So, here we are…right smack-dab in the middle of a hero's journey that we did not even have on our calendars. We're not even sure when this calendar entry will end, let alone what is expected of us during this 24/7 six-month (plus) event (as of this book's launch).

In the early days of *The Pause*, many of us went into survival mode. We stocked the house with food, medication, necessities (toilet paper, chocolate?!)… whatever we felt we could not absolutely, positively live without. *The Pause* began to wear thin on some of us…it would not go away…and it soon became our new normal. My new normal evolved into an ever-evolving process of what I now call my time to "Review, Rethink, and Reimagine"…

Review

With *The Pause* came the gift of time…time that I could fill however I wanted. In the beginning, I found myself using my new time to review what "works" and what doesn't work. I took a look at both home and office functionality and began to clear out whatever was not working and began replacing it with something different…something better. I have learned to literally "let it go." I hated my office chair as it hurt my back to sit in for very long. I sold the old chair and found a new (for me), refurbished one on sale at an office furniture recycler that was much more comfortable. I also recognized that I needed to build a stronger, more stable bookkeeping system and began the search for new, reliable resources to fill that void. At home, I started going through a stack of old storage boxes in our basement and either selling, giving, or donating carloads of junk—I've been in total, full-out purge mode. If it wasn't working for me or serving the greater good of the household (or business), it has been released and let go.

Rethink

Being in *The Pause* has allowed me to rethink processes, old patterns, and old habits. Whether at home or in our business, I've been given the chance to fix what's broken, mend misunderstandings, and adjust old thought patterns. I've been given the gift of more time to think things through; more time to ask for opinions, new ideas, or suggestions on how to do things differently. I've learned "auto-pilot" is not a speed, it's an avoidance mechanism. I am the only one who makes up my deadlines; that means I can change them! I can rethink my week and schedule in my own personal "time-outs"!

Reimagine

The Pause is the "Big Kahuna," folks. It's up to us, whether we imagine ourselves riding on top of the wave or letting it pull us under. Before *The Pause*, our hero's journey was all wrapped up in our personal achievements. Whether we were trying to build a successful business, raise a happy family, plan a vacation, or produce a work of art, these all represented external achievements. *The Pause* is asking us to turn our focus inward—into our homes, into our authentic selves. It is through this change in focus that we become more aware and more conscious; and as our journey transitions to an emphasis on internal growth, we are being led into transformation.

You are here. Right now. On purpose. For a reason.

Although it may not feel all that pleasant, we have all been called to this adventure, at this particular time, for our own unique reasons. The future holds the promise of a new beginning, and we have been summoned to make a positive impact as we begin to mold a new earth.

We are the ones who hold the magic—the magic-fairy sparkle dust—that is so desperately needed right now to rebuild.

We are the ones who are willing to extend a hand, share our treasures, and reach out to others in need.

We are the ones needed NOW—to not only offer compassion, comfort, and consolation, but to also initiate dialogue and direction.

You, too, are the light—the one who can shine and light the way for others. Yours is the light so desperately needed NOW—to rebuild communities, confidence, and broken dreams.

It is time for you to shine so that others may draw hope, strength, and courage from YOUR light and learn to let their own light shine.

It is you. You have chosen to accept this mission…at this time…on this planet.

You are a Bright Spot.

Cathy Davis is founder/CEO of Davis Creative Publishing Partners. After a corporate career as a creative director at Bank of America Trust, Cathy struck out on her own in January of 2004. Originally offering branding and design Services, Cathy pivoted the company in support of authors in 2007. The Davis Creative Publishing Partners division now helps speakers, trainers, consultants, and experts use the power of publishing as a marketing tool to grow their businesses. Cathy's husband, Jack, joined the company in 2008 after almost 20 years at Fleishman-Hillard, a global public relations firm. Together, they now use their decades of experience as visual and verbal communicators to help their clients reap the benefits of publishing for both personal and business growth.

cathy@daviscreative.com
www.DavisCreative.com
www.linkedin.com/in/cathyldavis/
www.facebook.com/DavisCreativeLLC
www.youtube.com/channel/UC5L1yOYzT0gPP-tXY02ltVA
www.instagram.com/cathyl.davis/

Choose to Move Forward and SHINE!

In times of crisis—in our country, our world, or in our personal and professional lives—what we stand for gets brought into stark relief, calling us to make choices about the values that are most important to us. Our personal boundaries get tested, and we have the choice to answer the challenge by keeping our boundaries clear and strong.

I've been seeing people bumping against their boundaries during the pandemic, buffeted back and forth by worry, fear, constant news of disaster and scarcity. They give in to the negativity they feel all around them and shrink back in their businesses and lives. Their boundaries around their values, ambitions, and goals become blurred by other people's messages of fear about the future.

When we put our energy into those fears, more fear is created. We keep on attracting the same, and we continue to shrink and contract instead of expanding and sharing ourselves out into the world. We make small decisions, afraid to struggle and to take risks that will support us in following our big dreams. I am seeing this shrinking happen in business. I believe fear is causing new projects to be dropped, prices to be slashed, future plans and strategies to be paused.

The pulling back that fear is causing lights a fire in my belly, a passion that has me stand up and shout, "No!" I am not willing to entertain negativity and fear! I am holding strong to my boundaries, taking a stand for MOVING FORWARD. I know that it's hard. But what is so clear to me from this pandemic is that it doesn't mean we stop and/or contract. We can still choose to move forward—we *have* to move forward. We cannot allow difficult times to have us shrink back.

We are in this together and the world needs us most when the challenges are greatest.

My choice is to move forward purposefully. I have a whole company of people—and clients—whom I am not going to let down. I'm not willing to entertain anything less. In fact, I want to see how much we can do, how many lives we can touch for good. More than ever, we need to stand firm, to believe in what we do, to lean in and bring it forward, powerfully and positively.

It's absolutely the time to step forward and be visible, to shine!

Being bright spots in the world means choosing what we believe in and what we're shining FOR. It means choosing what our boundaries are so we can stand firm and lift others up to move things in a positive direction.

In a crisis situation when there are people who are struggling and need support, we need those bright lights. We need people standing up, showing up, helping move the economy and society and the world forward.

During these challenging times, I am continuing to move forward in the ways that I am being called to serve. I continue to offer and expand my services, still charging for them but working closely with people to find ways for them to move forward as well. I am choosing to meet people where they are and honor their choices while keeping my boundaries. I couldn't do this if I were entertaining a mindset of fear and scarcity.

In every conversation, we have the opportunity to lift up, support, and really listen to others. We can make the choice to be positive and forward-thinking, to be generous with our connections and introductions. We can choose abundance thinking by sharing our gifts and connections.

If you see a connection that can serve, don't think about what's in it for you. Think: Wow! If I brought these two amazing people together, what great things might be created! And you know what? You will feel good at the end of the day. You will be looking less at what you're struggling with and more at what you are being honored to experience. When you make the choice to stand with your boundaries, you are attracting love and possibility, instead of buying into fear and scarcity.

What are you choosing to entertain?
What are you choosing to accept?

It becomes time to draw that line for yourself. What are you choosing to accept and entertain? What are you choosing to let go? What are you spending your energy on right now? Is it meaningful and serving your purpose and values? Are you moving forward with purpose and positivity?

We do not need to change our boundaries or values out of fear.

As I'm watching what is happening worldwide, and in our country, I am looking for the good that I can choose to entertain, to reflect on, and to celebrate. I'm looking for what can unite us instead of divide us. I'm looking for ways to bring forward health, healing, vibrancy, and collaboration.

What are the positive things that you can see in the world?

When we choose to see things more positively, we see struggles differently. I am not pretending that things aren't hard. My dad always says: "Hard is not a reason not to." I didn't really like hearing this. Sometimes things are hard. You don't stop because something is difficult. We need to be willing to push through, to move things that matter to us forward.

What do you stand for? What are you entertaining? What are you choosing to bring forward? Are you choosing to tear down greatness in others or celebrate it?

The shift to move forward starts with each of us. Choose to stand in your values. Stand for what matters to you, celebrate the greatness in yourself and others. Choose to shine brightly out into the world. Heart by heart, life by life, together we can bring light, encouragement, joy, and hope to the world! Be the bright light you can be and SHINE!

Rebecca Hall Gruyter is a global influencer, No. 1 International Bestselling and award-winning author, compiler, in-demand publisher, popular radio show host (listeners on over eight networks), and an empowerment leader. She has built multiple platforms to help experts and influencers reach more people. These platforms include radio, TV, books, magazines, the Speaker Talent Search, and live events, creating a powerful promotional reach of over ten million people!

Rebecca is the CEO of RHG Media Productions, which has helped 200-plus authors become best sellers! She has personally contributed to twenty-five-plus published books, multiple magazines, and has been quoted in Major Media, The Huffington Post, ABC, CBS, NBC, Fox, and Thrive Global. She has been recognized as one of the top-ten working women in America by AWWIN, Inc. She now helps experts to have great impact and become quoted in major media.

Be Seen, Heard and SHINE!

www.YourPurposeDrivenPractice.com
www.RHGTVNetwork.com
www.SpeakerTalentSearch.com
Rebecca@YourPurposeDrivenPractice.com

The Heart Knows

Failure has been a theme throughout my life since high school, a lesson the universe gifted me time and time again. Unfortunately, I wasn't listening and didn't hear the synchronicities in my path. Sometimes we cannot see what is right in front of us; we do not see gifts but criticism, failure, and fear.

From Don McLean, "the day the music died," I was a young college musician—classical organ. When I was dismissed from the program and not allowed to continue, there was no warning, there was no plan B. My world just stopped. My professor walked out of my practice room and my life changed forever. I can still hear the door click as he walked out of the room, leaving me in wonder about a future I never saw.

Many people were well meaning, saying things like, "It wasn't meant to be" or "Just let it go." But they didn't tell me how. Eventually, I learned.

My initial response was that of a petulant teenager, "If you don't want me, I don't want you." I ran away and didn't look back. I put my fears in a box and placed the box in the back of the closet for more than thirty years. I didn't deal with it. I didn't face it. I didn't unwrap it. I left it to fester in my subconscious where it severely impacted my world.

Life is energy and failure deposited negative energy in my body until I was forced to deal. The clues had always been there; my subconscious silenced them each time until there was no longer an option. This dark energy drained my body and made me sick, forcing me into a wheelchair for nine months.

One day the universe forced my hand in a surprise move. When we do the hard work, solutions present themselves.

When I moved back to my hometown after my divorce to be near my eighty-plus-year-old parents, the universe began sending messages. I had not been home in more than twenty-five years. My life was about to come full circle. It was time.

The messenger the universe sent was music.

In November 2019, a family interviewed candidates to find a home for their beloved 30-year-old baby grand piano. She came home with me and my world changed again.

I remember the day the piano was delivered. After they unwrapped the baby grand piano and put in my great room, I sat at the piano bench with my hands on the keyboard. I remained afraid. It was like meeting a lost love in the dark, wondering how to reach out for the first time…

I relived that fateful moment in college. I remembered the anger; I felt the disappointment and the pain. I heard that fateful click of the door closing…

I opened the top of the piano and began to play. It was as if I was saying hello to an old friend. I could feel the emotions in my hands and throughout my body as the chains in my heart began to soften. The tears began to fall. I began to shake. My body slowly released the negative energy held painfully for decades.

The process was slow. I was an organist, not a pianist—the technique is very different. I had to relearn reading music: left hand, right hand, treble clef, bass clef, touch, volume… So many things came flooding back all at once.

Slam. I closed the piano top. I was overwhelmed and could not fully process the tidal wave of emotions. I stopped. It took several days before I could return.

I learned to invite music back into my life slowly at first. Being a musician is not what you do; it is who you are. The emotions flooded back with such a paradox. Joy replaced sorrow. Happiness replaced anger. Forgiveness replaced pain.

The path home was an inward one, a journey many find too painful to begin. For me, letting go meant sitting at the piano in quiet moments to listen to my heart. My head is often the driver of my life, but the secret was in quieting the mind to hear my heart speak.

The love of music came back. Initially, I had to sit and simply be. I didn't play. I listened. I was still. It was in these moments I learned to forgive myself for not seeing the gift my professor gave me many decades ago.

As each day passed, music returned to heal my heart; a healing I never thought possible. As my heart began to heal, so did my body. I experienced the chains slowly releasing one-by-one until they no longer chained me to a failure that happened so long ago. Music healed me from the inside out. I had to open that gift from the past to heal my future. Music found me and saved my life. I finally found the courage to open the box of fears in the back of the closet. Joy filled my life once again, opening opportunities to heal other areas of my life.

The lesson? To move faster, we need to slow down. To move forward, we need to move inward. Answers are found in the quiet moments when we listen to our heart. To let go means to be still, to listen to what our body already knows. Letting go means forgiveness of self.

Only when we go within can peace be truly achieved.

Courage was in taking the first step. I first had to learn to trust that I was on the right path and trust that I always had the abilities to heal within.

There are no short cuts. We cannot hide the box away and expect healing. Only when we are ready is the universe a patient teacher waiting for us to begin.

Believe in yourself. Know that your heart knows and will take you the rest of the way home.

Known as the "Academic Entrepreneur," Dr. Cheryl Lentz connects with audiences as a unique and dynamic speaker who has one foot in academia and one foot in business and entrepreneurial spaces. Her goal is to offer the participants pearls of wisdom today that they can use tomorrow in their personal and professional lives.

Known globally for her writings on leadership and failure, as well as critical and refractive thinking, she has been published more than forty-four times with twenty-five writing awards. As an accomplished university professor, speaker, and consultant, she is an international best-selling author, as well as top-quoted publishing professional on ABC, CBS, NBC, and Fox. She will take the stage as a TEDx speaker in *Farmingdale2020 on October 10, 2020.

Join Dr. Cheryl on her journey to provide audiences with inspiration, knowledge, and counsel to move forward effectively.

www.DrCherylLentz.com
www.twitter.com/drcheryllentz
www.linkedin.com/in/drcheryllentz/
www.refractivethinker.com/
www.drcheryllentz.com/
www.facebook.com/Dr.Cheryl.Lentz

The Other Side of Change

During the late nineties, I held a senior vice president title and had been with the bank thirteen years. At the time, the banking industry was going through merger mania. Job security was nonexistent. Back then, separation packages were generous. So what do you do? You ask to be fired of course!

Having two babies at home, a one- and a four-year-old, I wanted to have more control in my life; I wanted to be a mom first. We were a two-income family, and we needed my income to survive the New Jersey cost of living. My solution was to open my own business.

My supportive husband said, "Go for it."

I am a calculated risk-taker. To start my business, I had to calculate: (1) risk—not having a secure paycheck; (2) potential reward—freedom with kids and control over my income and career; (3) educated risk—an MBA in finance and, at that time, nineteen years in sales with a huge network of people who I could reach out to; and, finally, (4) work ethic—an ability to create opportunity by being tenacious, ethical, authentic, and organized with my business plan of attack.

Funny how we can look back and see the processes we create for building a successful and happy life. What I learned twenty years ago when I requested to be fired from banking helped me once the pandemic hit this year and my income stopped.

When change hits, how do you get through it and come out the other side better, stronger, wiser, happier?

TIPS

Self-reflect—I went back to my formula of identifying risk/reward/educated risk/work ethic before moving forward. It's interesting to self-reflect and realize that life is more planned than we often think. The funny thing is I had no idea I used a formulated plan twenty years ago that would serve me today!

How many of you self-reflect and see opportunities using superpowers you have developed over the years? Kind of a fun exercise (just don't get stuck there)!

Opportunities are everywhere. The trick is knowing which opportunities to exploit and which to walk away from. My formula in a nutshell:

- Step 1—Identify the risk of the situation at hand: in this case the pandemic, no income, and the potential upside (or downside) of spending money on business growth with no income.
- Step 2—Shine a light of pure logic and park your heart/fear! That means put your heart and emotional responses aside so you can control and minimize fear that may debilitate you from seeing the situation or opportunity clearly and may hold you back from a great new opportunity. This is not an easy step!
- Step 3—Educate yourself to understand the new situation, the technology being used; see the true potential/options/opportunities, the costs to move forward, and the time frame to execute before making an educated decision.
- Step 4—Ask people outside of the situation to help you explore the options and opportunities. LISTEN to and pursue their perspectives; they may see things that may save time and money; they may even connect you with the right people. We all have blind spots, and as I say: "You don't know what you don't know, until someone shines a light on the situation. Then you can't unknow what you just learned. You can either choose to use or not use the information. Choose wisely!"
- Step 5—Use your brain and research, then trust your gut. You need to hone your gut-reaction skills. My gut has served me well for the past fifty-eight years!!

The pandemic hit and the world spun like a top, a game to test us, to see who landed and who flew away. With that spin came tremendous new opportunities. Did you see new opportunities?

So what options did I evaluate early in 2020 to make an educated decision to move forward and thrive during the pandemic? I hired a team to update my website and social media; to rebrand my business; to start a second division of my company, Whitman & Associates, LLC; and to start building a digital library of my sales courses that I had used in my live training.

I had no income, yet bills for these services were pouring in. I was at a huge crossroad. Do I keep moving forward or do I stop? This was a tough one. I had my normal household, business, and college expenses to keep up with (my kids did grow up after all). Do I keep spending money on building another division in my business?

I, again, went back to my formula. Identifying the risk was hard since there were so many unknown variables due to the lack of information with the pandemic. My logic was screaming, "Now, more than ever, digital and online courses for training are needed." I needed to keep moving forward.

I stepped back and educated myself so I could see the options and the upside potential. I looked at what I was creating with my digital footprint, and began building an online membership platform with all my courses digitized (How does "Whitman University" sound? I am open to suggestions for my new membership class site!!). I began my research and listened to other experts who were pursuing the same new frontier I was venturing into. What success were they having? What did they see as new opportunities in this changing world of Zoom interactions?

I read, joined online Masterclasses, and group trainings. I joined several five- and six-day intensive workshops, and I worked longer hours. The learning was fun and exciting.

As I write this chapter the world is opening back up. I can say that I did move forward during the pandemic: a book launch is scheduled for July 16, 2020; my digital classes and membership site are scheduled to go live August of 2020. Using my formula worked yet again! I have come out on the other side!

Are you feeling the shift and coming out the other side better, stronger, wiser, happier?

A high-energy, passionate, and enthusiastic teacher and coach, Connie Whitman helps ambitious business owners, leaders, and sales teams build powerhouse organizations to achieve outrageous goals.

An international speaker, podcast host, and influencer, Connie's inspired teaching, transformational tools, and content ensure that business owners and salespeople grow their revenue streams through internal and external communication skills, while developing strong relationship-based cultures.

Connie has been the CEO of Whitman & Associates, LLC for two-decades. Her signature 7-Step Sales Process has helped thousands of sales people grow their businesses to high six-figure incomes. She is a trusted strategic partner who builds lasting relationships with business owners, thought leaders, and organizations worldwide.

As a podcast host, she shares inspiring content on her weekly, international podcast, "Enlightenment of Change" (http://webtalkradio.net/internet-talk-radio/enlightenment-of-change/), a free resource for professionals looking to fast track their careers.

www.whitmanassoc.com/
Connie@whitmanassoc.com
www.facebook.com/WhitmanAndAssociates
www.linkedin.com/in/conniewhitman/
www.twitter.com/Connie_Whitman
Free Communication Style Assessment (CSA): www.whitmanassoc.com/csa

CHERYL BONINI ELLIS

Preparing for the Inevitable

Learning to manage energy and boost resilience can save your life. And like the best time to plant a tree was twenty years ago and the second-best time is today, now is the time to make the personal commitment to invest in your energy and resilience.

Life has a way of testing us to our limits. We don't know when—or even how—we will be called upon to show up as our best selves; we know that it is inevitable. A wise man said, "That which is most painful is most universal." The story of human existence is a story of pain and personal struggle. It's the thing we all have in common.

My opportunity to learn this lesson first-hand came when my husband was diagnosed with a rare form of cancer. I was thrust into the role of chief caretaker, morale booster, resident expert on treatment options, and navigator of a mystifying healthcare industry in the midst of change. I didn't ask for this. I didn't train for it. Nursing was not my calling. And yet, the love of my life was scared and vulnerable; he was counting on me to step up and be there. I didn't hesitate. I needed to re-prioritize my life.

Taking on all that was "new" required more energy than living my life, as I had known it before. And I realized that in order to see us through this crisis, I would have to protect my own health and well-being.

Here's the point: We never know when we will be called upon to step up in a big way, to stretch beyond our comfort zones, our training and experiences, even our vision of what our lives should be. So, think of learning to boost resilience as preparing for the inevitable. At some point, we will need to generate extra energy to support ourselves or someone we love through a challenge or hardship. And if we have done the work to build each of the four sources of energy—that is, physical, mental, emotional, and spiritual—we will be able to tap into a higher level of resilience needed to perform under pressure.

As a High-Performance Coach, I have realized that managing energy, all four sources, will increase productivity far more than managing time. And it is energy—rather than time—that becomes our most precious resource, so much so that it's been called the "currency of high performance." The energy-management tools and techniques I teach make the biggest difference in my clients' daily and weekly productivity, while preventing fatigue and burnout.

Fortunately, those four forms of energy work together synergistically, and working on any one of them also benefits the others. Have you ever noticed how physical exercise boosts your mood and your mental alertness? Or how accomplishing a difficult task that requires focus and attention increases your self-esteem and makes you feel better about yourself? This is multi-tasking, synergizing, in the best way.

Building our resilience and energy capacity is like strengthening our muscles. It requires a balance of expending energy and renewing energy. It means moving beyond our limits and then taking time to replenish through rituals, which we can adopt, that will enable this increase in energy capacity.

Of the four sources of energy, physical is the one we tend to focus on the most, because when we are fatigued and burned out, we can't seem to perform. Physical stamina grows when we apply rituals, such as getting plenty of sleep and sufficient hydration, eating a healthy diet, and exercising our bodies. All these things improve brain health, which contributes to our mental energy.

One of my favorite productivity enhancers may sound counterintuitive, that is, taking frequent short breaks throughout the day—stretching for five minutes, focusing on breathing, drinking some water, walking around, interacting with others—which allows for a quick reset and recovery. Clients who follow this advice report getting more done in less time with energy to spare at the end of a productive day.

Mental energy capacity can be enhanced with a positive optimistic outlook and attitude. Becoming aware of our inner dialogue, noting when it's negative and critical, replacing that with positive self-talk, can enhance our emotional and spiritual well-being as well. Add visualization and affirmations to the mix and we have a cocktail for boosting our mental energy.

Have you noticed how contagious emotions are? If we are surrounded by negativity, it's easy to get dragged into the fray. Positive emotions are equally contagious and critical to healthy relationships, work environments, and overall performance.

Positive emotional energy influences our emotional intelligence, which is often cited as a more important determinant of leadership success than IQ. The EQ (emotional quotient) components of self-awareness, self-control, empathy, and interpersonal effectiveness are essential elements of good leaders. Practicing positive habits, like patience, compassion, gratitude, and joy, will build those habits into supportive skills over time.

Spiritual energy stems from tapping into our core values, which, in turn, fuels passion. Honesty, integrity, and courage are spiritual traits that are fundamental to our humanity and critical to our existence. When we are able to connect to a purpose beyond our own self-interests, we are more committed and better able to persevere in the face of challenge. We've all observed how the energy of the human spirit can overcome even the direst circumstances—like helping someone we love through a life-threatening illness.

For me, the story has a happy ending. My husband and I made it through the crisis. His life was saved. And I learned some valuable lessons about keeping things in perspective. My life was also saved.

A tip for you: Start today to focus more time and attention on becoming physically energized, mentally focused, emotionally connected, and spiritually aligned. Building all your sources of energy will boost your level of resilience—that is, the ability to get back up after you get knocked down, again and again.

And that can save your life.

Cheryl Bonini Ellis is the author of *Becoming Deliberate: Changing the Game of Leadership from the Inside Out*. As a former senior executive turned entrepreneur, she has helped countless leaders achieve breakthrough success. She is a Certified High-Performance Leadership Coach, specializing in helping growth-minded business owners and executives build fully engaged, cohesive, high-performing teams.

Cheryl is a Founding Member of John Maxwell's Team of Coaches, Trainers and Speakers; a Certified Facilitator for 5 Behaviors of a Cohesive Team™, Everything DiSC™, Productive Conflict™, and PXT Select™. She is an adjunct faculty member for the Leadership Development Institute at Eckerd College, a network associate of The Center for Creative Leadership.

Cheryl currently resides in St. Petersburg, Florida.
cheryl@ellisbusinessenterprises.com
www.cherylboniniellis.com
www.linkedin.com/in/cherylboniniellis/
www.facebook.com/CherylBoniniEllis
www.instagram.com/cherylbonini/
www.youtube.com/results?search_query=cherylboniniellis
www.twitter.com/cabonini

Bringing Light to the Darkness

"Darkness cannot drive out darkness; only light can do that. Hate cannot drive out hate; only love can do that."
— Dr. Martin Luther King

Perhaps there never was a time more than now when we needed to be reminded of those words.

As the mother of a son who has an extremely rare chromosome disorder, I am used to operating in Plan B. But I do not think anyone, no matter what they had been dealing with prior, was prepared for this pandemic.

It had already been a tough couple years for us. My husband had taken a new job that involved commuting from St. Louis to Chicago. I was in my second year teaching at an all-girls high school. That year, I contracted both whooping cough and bronchitis. I tried not to focus on the stress, but on the good, which included friendships, family connections, and learning. The following fall, I started a new job at a university. It was challenging, but I focused on the many positives and used the forty-minute commute to catch up with news and friends.

I am not sure who said it first, but I reminded myself then, and even now, that "happiness is an inside job." As difficult as it has been, accepting that I am in control of my own happiness has been very freeing. This is illustrated in Eckhart Tolle's book *The Power of Now* when he says that no matter what is happening, we have three choices: (1) walk away, (2) work to change it, or (3) accept it fully. To accept the moment fully is always the possible—although often difficult—one. But doing so can help to bring light to even the darkest moments.

Blaise Pascal, a mathematician and philosopher said, "All of humanity's problems stem from man's inability to sit quietly in a room alone." If we can be happy "AllOne," as I call it, we have a tool for accepting darkness.

During spring "break" this year, my university administration made the decision to close campus and move courses online. Thereafter, my husband returned from Chicago and our two daughters came home from their respective colleges, all with only enough clothes for two weeks, thinking they would be back soon.

I went from being alone with our son to having everyone home at once. Of course, I was happy that my family was safe and well. But to say we had adjustments is a major understatement.

In order to stay grounded, I continued a practice I had started a few years ago: that is, beginning each day with Bible and Al-Anon readings, such as *Just for Today:*

JUST FOR TODAY I will try to live through this day only, and not tackle all my problems at once. I can do something for twelve hours that would appall me if I felt that I had to keep it up for a lifetime.

JUST FOR TODAY I will be happy. This assumes to be true what Abraham Lincoln said, that "Most folks are as happy as they make up their minds to be."

JUST FOR TODAY I will adjust myself to what is, and not try to adjust everything to my own desires. I will take my "luck" as it comes, and fit myself to it.

JUST FOR TODAY I will try to strengthen my mind. I will study. I will learn something useful. I will not be a mental loafer. I will read something that requires effort, thought, and concentration.

JUST FOR TODAY I will exercise my soul in three ways: I will do somebody a good turn, and not get found out; if anybody knows of it, it will not count. I will do at least two things I don't want to do—just for exercise. I will not show anyone that my feelings are hurt; they may be hurt, but today I will not show it.

JUST FOR TODAY I will be agreeable. I will look as well as I can, dress becomingly, keep my voice low, be courteous, criticize not one bit. I won't find fault with anything, nor try to improve or regulate anybody but myself.

JUST FOR TODAY I will have a program. I may not follow it exactly, but I will have it. I will save myself from two pests: hurry and indecision.

JUST FOR TODAY I will have a quiet half hour all by myself, and relax. During this half hour, sometime, I will try to get a better perspective of my life.

JUST FOR TODAY I will be unafraid. Especially, I will not be afraid to enjoy what is beautiful, and to believe that as I give to the world, so the world will give to me *(Just for Today,* Al-Anon Family Groups, Al-Anon Family Group Headquarters, Inc., 1600 Corporate Landing Parkway, Virginia Beach, VA 23454-5617, 14-75 M-10).

These principles are often hard to apply. But reading them through the pandemic created daily goals, and I looked at the bright side, bringing light to the darkness. That is:

- Instead of being frustrated at the increase of laundry, I said a prayer of gratitude that my whole family was home.
- Instead of complaining that I was shopping, cooking, and cleaning all the time, I was grateful that I was able to do all three and that we could afford to do so.
- Instead of complaining about my job, I was thankful that I still had a job.
- Instead of thinking of it as another chore, I took lunch to my husband, upstairs in his home office, every day, thankful that he no longer had the commute that had brought him so much stress.
- Instead of being negative, I made a gratitude list. If I had trouble with the list, I went through the alphabet, such as "A" for apple. "I am grateful I have an apple to eat."
- Instead of complaining and holding resentment, I found fun ways to look for an anonymous good deed. Sometimes it was as "simple" as putting away someone's socks or underwear left on the counter. (Say what!)

Of course, I am not always able to apply these principles or to be grateful, but when I am, everything is brighter. If each of us would focus on ourselves, then each of us could be a candle in the darkness.

Think of how bright the world would be then!

Dr. Theresa Jeevanjee teaches computer science and mathematics at Lindenwood University and for MEGSSS (Mathematics Education for Gifted Secondary School Students). She enjoys running, painting, cooking, and taking ballet classes.

Theresa is an associate in the CSJ (Congregation of St. Joseph) community and is active in two prayer groups. Her volunteer work includes tutoring mathematics, helping with the theatre and chorus costumes for her daughter's high school, and helping her neighborhood and parish.

She and her husband live in Webster Groves, Missouri, with their children, Ryan, Kiran, and Lauren, and their dog, Kuki Monster.

tjeevanjee@gmail.com
faithandrelentlesslove.com

BILL ELLIS

Let's See Where This Journey Takes Us!

He had considered it for weeks. Should he go—or not? It was a conference featuring a powerful list of speakers. He was a coach affiliated with the event's host, Bob Burg. He should go. But he was struggling to end a difficult relationship. He didn't want to socialize, nor create any drama. Go just for the business, he decided.

She too had contemplated whether or not to make the journey to south Florida, facing her own challenges at the time. Hers would be a more arduous journey as she lived in Dubai. She'd connected with Bob via Twitter, through *The Go-Giver*, a book he'd co-authored and one that had been a foundational influence on her business. Her decision? Go. Meet Bob. Hear the speakers. Gain a new life experience.

Neither of them had any idea of the blessing that awaited them.

He decided to make an appearance at the event's welcome event, feeling comfortable as part of a small group speaking with his friend, mentor, and conference host. It was then that he first spotted her as she walked to the poolside event.

"Wow," he thought. There's something about that woman—her looks, her manner, how people were drawn to her. She ordered a glass of wine, then started towards his group. He felt a bit anxious, even though it was clear her purpose was to meet Bob.

He and she also met. Her energy was palpable. Her conversation engaging. Her travel to the conference unique. For his part, he reminded himself, "Business only."

The two crossed paths again the next morning during a break. They exchanged warm greetings and a brief hug, discussed their take on the morning's speakers, then returned to their seats at opposite sides of the room.

Their next encounter was through social media—connecting on LinkedIn and Twitter. They exchanged emails, realizing that there was something between them, a spark of sorts, that ensured their communication would continue.

Emails led to phone calls and then to her returning to the U.S. to spend time with him and experience a new city. The initial spark had grown into a flame. There was a definite connection that both chose to explore further. Their relationship continued to blossom in spite of the 7,512-mile distance, different cultural backgrounds, and the residual impact from his now-ended relationship.

He visited her in Dubai—his first international travel in decades. He realized that not only was she truly special, but that his world was also broadening at a dizzying pace. Seeing the Middle East first-hand allowed him to smash much of the misinformation he'd been exposed to throughout his life. The people there were just like those in his city—love of family and hard work, all seeking happiness and security.

They began to discuss their potential future together. One day, his comments went something like, "There are so many challenges for us. I have twin granddaughters whom I won't leave. Your children are in Dubai. You have a thriving business there; mine is in the States." No doubt he highlighted a few more obstacles.

Not surprisingly, her perspective was different. Her response? "Why are you creating roadblocks that don't yet exist? They may become reality, and we'll address them if they do. In the meantime, I ask that you join me on this journey, and let's see where it takes us!"

"I'm in!" he thought.

They recognized that what they had was truly special. Their relationship was unique in its geographic distance, but more so in the intensity of the love they shared. Focusing on positives, working to accommodate differences, and simply being grateful, allowed their love to grow deeper.

Both had their lives broadened, gaining new cultural perspectives. They travelled to places neither had been, but also to cities where one shared their experience with the other: Paris, New York, London, Chicago, Oman, Memphis, Georgia (both country and state), Beirut, Orlando, Bucharest, and Oklahoma

City. They visited New Orleans, his hometown, and South Africa, the country in which she was raised.

They travelled back and forth between the United Arab Emirates and the U.S. They learned early to set a firm date for their next meeting before leaving each other. Doing so gave them a countdown, "thirty days," "twenty-nine days," "twenty-eight days…." providing hope, building anticipation, and reminding them they'd be reunited soon.

Four years after meeting, they were married in St. Louis. Her children and his, the twin granddaughters, and an eclectic gathering of friends celebrated the union in a small nineteenth-century stone church.

They celebrated their four-year anniversary and New Year's 2020 together in the U.S. He made a short trip to Dubai in February, and she did the same to the States, returning home on March 10th. Just days later, the world plunged into a pandemic, the likes of which had not been seen since 1918.

International travel was virtually halted. Their countdown of twenty-five days quickly became irrelevant. The uncertainty brought on by the pandemic and not knowing when they'd reunite was a challenge they'd not before encountered.

Lockdowns and stay-at-home orders in both their cities increased their level of anxiety—isolated from their normal activities and by the universal fear present just below everyone's consciousness.

Fueled by their faith in brighter times to come, the couple committed to staying connected via phone and video. They shared pictures every day titled "Today's memory," celebrating past joys and the promise of their future. They adopted a new approach to counting: "One day closer!" Their motto? "Stay in the day!"

Finally, a brief window opened for international travel allowing her to fly to Chicago. He made the five-hour drive to meet her, thereby eliminating an additional flight to St. Louis and any additional risk it presented. After 111 days, they were reunited.

Uncertainties still exist. However, this couple has lived a life of happiness and fulfillment based on a simple credo, "Be grateful, address roadblocks as they appear, and let's see where this journey takes us!"

Bill Ellis is a master at unlocking the fearless potential in others. A veteran of corporate brand management for more than twenty-five years at global beverage giant Anheuser-Busch, Bill has come to learn and deliver his true value in the past decade as a public speaker, certified coach, and brand architect for individuals and businesses.

His blog, *Friday's Fearless Brand*, profiles successful people, places and organizations, and has served as the foundation for *Women Who Won*, a book sparked by Bill's twin granddaughters and his wish for their happy future as successful, intrepid women. It is his hope that the compilation of stories of amazing women from all walks of life will inspire and remind—men and women—that we all can win.

A devoted father, grandfather, and husband to Tara Rogers-Ellis, Bill divides his time between St. Louis, Missouri, and Dubai, United Arab Emirates.

bill@brandingforresults.com
www.brandingforresults.com
www.brandingpillars.com
www.linkedin.com/in/wcellis
www.facebook.com/bill.ellis

MARY NUNALEY

Living Your Outrageous Idea

Have you ever felt the urge to do something outrageous? Perhaps it was skydiving or traveling the world alone or maybe starting your own business? The urge to start my own business was something that nagged me for years until I finally decided the time was right to go out on a limb, walk away from corporate life, and see what I could do on my own. Little did I know how many changes would occur in two and a half years.

I've got some ideas I'd like to share and you might want to try when you are ready to do something outrageous? Are you ready?

A little back story. I've always been the one to color outside the lines, but I also like structure and stability. As a single mom, working full-time, homeschooling, and raising two athletes, structure was key for all of the family to succeed. And I was willing to be a bit different—heck, working full-time and homeschooling is not the norm! By 2012, I had raised two pretty competent humans, one of whom is now my business partner. To succeed in this less traditional approach to life, it took creativity, tenacity, and a willingness to accept help from others.

Think about a challenging time in your life. Write down five traits that helped you get through that time. This will help you as you focus on your outrageous idea!

The year 2018 arrived and I began my entrepreneurial journey. I had planned to freelance and pick up jobs that excited me, projects that allowed me to use my creativity and design skills, and bring some fun to traditionally humdrum corporate online training. Then, my son quit his job and said, "Mom, I want to join the family business." Hmm, plot twist. Good news. I knew his skills and his limitations, so we created a plan for how he could contribute. I explained that he had to earn his keep, but that I would provide training. That first year was pretty rough as he learned more about what he liked and didn't like about working in an online business. The first six months in business was all about belt-tightening, frugality, and taking any work that came our way—any work. It was okay. We were developing a foundation, learning more about the type of work and ideal clients we wanted to focus on.

How does this apply to your outrageous idea? Sometimes, your idea is vague and you aren't clear on what your end result should be. My suggestion: Create two lists related to your outrageous idea: one, things that excite you; two, things that drag you down. Now, go test some of those ideas and see if they really do excite you. If not, it's okay to move them to the drag-you-down column. It's all about finding what's important.

As 2019 arrived, our work had paid off. We added several new clients, projects, and long-term commitments. We were able to take some chances and expand the business. We had an amazing year and were on track to break records in 2020. Hooray!

January 2020 arrived and we had great plans for the business. Over the year, our goals were to add three new clients, launch a gamification course, and continue the work we were doing for existing clients. The path seemed clear and we were riding high. Then, March 2020 and the global health crisis arrived. The bottom dropped out. Clients began to call saying, "You have done great work, but we're cutting budgets and…" You get the idea. Every project in the works stopped. We weren't alone, but we sure felt alone. We had two choices: sink into despair or take action. We chose to take action.

Have you ever had the bottom drop out from under you? What did you do when you received bad news? If you could go back in time, what, if anything, would you do differently? As you think about your outrageous idea, do you have a plan for success? What would that look like?

Action—it was our saving grace. As friends and colleagues shared how they were cleaning their houses, binge watching *Tiger King*,[1] or wondering what to do with their stay-at-home time, we used the quarantine as a chance to reflect and

---

1 Rebecca Chaiklin and Eric Goode, dir., Docuseries. Tiger King: Murder, Mayhem and Madness. 2020. Los Gatos, California: Netflix, 2020.

reset. It was time to look at the business and see how we could not only weather this storm but also future-proof for whatever might lie ahead. We did three things that opened the door for new opportunities and future success:

1. **Network. Network. Network.** We attended in-person networking meetings early in 2020, then switched to virtual meetings as the global crisis hit. I joined Facebook challenges that taught me new skills, expanded our network, and resulted in being interviewed on multiple podcasts about our courses, gamification, and explainer videos. I also joined a Mastermind group, comprised of like-minded folks from India, Switzerland, and Vietnam, which provided new points of view and new opportunities.

2. **Learn.** We dedicated one day per week to professional development, that is, mastering new skills and software, and reading industry-related books, which have now become a regular part of our business culture. Always be learning.

3. **Recharge.** This is one that seems strange, especially during a crisis. It's important to take time off to recharge. One technique that works for us is committing two days per week for meetings, three days for focused productivity and professional development, and two days to recharge. Dead batteries do not work.

What are three things you can do to help reach your outrageous idea? Are you ready to adjust to the challenges that may come your way?

All things considered, running a business and adjusting how we think, act, and perform during a global crisis have been the bright spots of my career. So be bold! Adjust, carry on, and thrive!

Mary Nunaley is an ATD certified Master Instructional Designer™ and award-winning course developer.

Along with her son, Amadeus, she started the Lavender Dragon Team to help small and medium businesses bring their online courses to life by creating engaging and interactive courses that put the fun back into learning.

Mary brings a sense of playfulness and passion to everything she does and is always asking why is this happening and how can we improve it? This comes through in the work she does with her clients and the impact they are able to make with their audiences.

Mary graduated with a Master's in Education from Cal State East Bay and a Bachelor's in History from DePaul University in Chicago. She is also an ATD certified eLearning developer.

marynunaley@lavenderdragonteam.com
www.linkedin.com/in/mary-nunaley
www.facebook.com/lavenderdragonteam
www.lavenderdragonteam.com

CAREN LIBBY

The Power of Personal Branding

It was 1997. The concept of personal branding debuted in "The Brand Called You,"1 an article that was written by business guru Tom Peters for *Fast Company Magazine*. He wrote, "If you want to grow your brand, you've got to come to terms with power—your own." It's a compelling directive that can inspire anyone to work towards becoming the best they can be by paying attention to and improving their personal brand.

That same year, I was living in Northern California where I started my first business as an independent sales representative in the gift industry. Growing my territory was dependent on the trusted relationships that I had created with my clients over a period of years. Rather than "cold call" on the owners and buyers, I became a familiar face by visiting them in their stores and sharing news about the industry or new products that might interest them. As those relationships grew, I began to study what made some of my customers more successful. It became apparent that the store owners who established a solid customer base spent years creating a unique brand that appealed to their audience. I also spent time helping them merchandise their displays and learned some of the tricks that made their businesses stand apart from the competition.

The interaction with my customers improved my sales, and I enjoyed my job much more. As a result of that educational experience, I organized the notes I had taken from interviews with my customers, and I conducted extensive research about the industry. The result was a handbook, *Pizzazz Works: The Magic of*

---

1 Tom Peters. "The Brand Called You." *Fast Company*, no. August/September, August 31, 1997.

Motivational Merchandising, which was published in 2005. It includes guides and helpful hints for small independent retailers.

The Bright Spot—Differentiating Your Brand

What I learned from this experience was how the value that successful business owners placed on their customers was related to their long-term success. They drew people into their stores by offering a welcoming environment and creative displays of their products. Each store had a personality that reflected what the owners had to offer. They hosted special events and nurtured relationships with local clientele over a period of years.

It was 2007. The Great Recession had begun. I had been working in sales and marketing for a large corporation in St. Louis, Missouri, my hometown, when the dominoes began to fall. Employee morale took a nosedive as we witnessed the layoffs of our colleagues almost daily. Rather than stand by and wait to see if I would be among them, I resigned from my position. Six months later, my entire department was outsourced.

In 2008, I started my second business, this time as a freelance photographer. For a year, I photographed individuals, families, and events on location. I began blogging and learned how to build websites and develop digital marketing programs. Going "digital" was a turning point, and that has been the core of my business to this day.

By 2009, our country was going through an economic upheaval that shifted the direction of the lives of millions of people. I was struggling with how to build my business in that environment when I heard about the opening of a new organization called "GO! Network." It had been created to help career professionals who needed direction, education, and connections. They asked the career professionals who attended to raise their hands if they wanted to volunteer to help develop the community. I was one of those people.

At our first meeting, the volunteers were asked to come up with ideas about how to run the organization, based on their expertise and goals. Ultimately, committees were formed to develop and manage specific responsibilities such as programming, marketing, budgeting, and event planning. I volunteered to lead the marketing committee and became a member of the planning board.

This volunteer position was a chance to give back, get engaged, and make good use of my time. Like the other people who showed up, I needed a village! I was interested in pursuing marketing as a full-time career, and this was an opportunity to learn more about it as I grew my network. During that time, I worked with writers, graphic designers, and members of the other committees on outreach and providing quality programs for the attendees. I also photographed many of the members as well as several events. The hands-on experience set the stage for a better future for those of us who chose to participate. As the community grew, the organization helped the members grow their personal brands, provided educational experiences, valuable connections, and career opportunities.

The Bright Spot—Growing with Your Community

Fortunately, the economy improved by 2011, and people found jobs or started businesses that were on the other side of this devastating period in our history. I'm still in contact with many of the people I met there, and what I learned took my business to another level. I joined other professional groups and continued to branch out and grow a profitable company. Building community through productive networking and volunteering has been a gift that will keep on giving now and forever.

It's been over twenty years since I started my entrepreneurial journey. Focusing on my own brand has been pivotal to my success because it's helped me understand how I can shine a spotlight on my clients. They come to me with their ideas, hopes, and dreams, and we work together to take them online so they can meet their goals. We work on developing their personal brand and how they can use it to come to terms with their own power.

No matter what is going on in the world, it's essential to reach within and focus on your goals. If you want to reignite your business, find the right job, achieve recognition, or attract new clients, creating or enhancing your personal brand is an excellent place to begin.

Caren Libby founded Image Media, LLC in 2008. Clients hire her to elevate their personal brand and transform their digital assets. She specializes in web design, digital marketing programs, and on-location photography. She is the author of *Pizzazz Works: The Magic of Motivational Merchandising,* a handbook for small independent retailers, that was published in 2005.

Caren's creative services are designed for entrepreneurs and small business owners who want to expand their audience and increase their sales. She is the creator of Build Business Studio, a comprehensive program for brand building, storytelling, and online content creation. Her background is in corporate and entrepreneurial marketing management, project management, and sales.

In addition to capturing her family, friends, nature, and neighborhoods, Caren has a passion for taking photographs of groups and individuals that tell their stories and showcase their personal brands.

www.Carenlibby.com
www.Linkedin.com/in/CarenLibby
www.Facebook.com/carenlibby
www.Twitter.com/carenlibby
www.Instagram.com/carenlibby

Happy Keys

We spend much of our lives in search of happiness. We look for it in relationships, careers, cars, homes, "ideal" body shapes, and more. When the global pandemic descended, followed by economic crisis, and then social uprising, fear of catastrophe followed and our collective happiness seemed threatened.

After months of sheltering in place, I experienced days of intense quarantine fatigue that felt heavy. I wondered if returning to "normal" would be possible or even desired. Mostly, I held tightly to a sense of gratitude.

> *"Don't put the keys to your happiness into someone else's pocket."*
> — Unknown

As someone who's pivoted from one relationship to another since her teens (including two marriages and long-term cohabitations), this quote resonates with me. It's a powerful reminder that even in our closest relationships, happiness must come from within. I believe the foundations of happiness are rooted in three components: health, self-care, and mindset.

Health

Perhaps the greatest silver lining of the 2020 pandemic is that it forced us into slowing our pace while inviting us to look inward. Sheltering in place has offered an opportunity to reconnect with ourselves, our families, and our values. We have reinvented and reflected. People have awakened to the importance of their health. Although for many, it has come with hardships and losses; accepting and embracing change is easier than resisting. The change came suddenly and it was outside our control, making it especially hard. But there's an opportunity for post-traumatic growth if we allow it.

"Hunk, Chunk, or Drunk." This poignant viral social media meme resonated with one of my wellness coaching clients. She adopted it as her "WhyPowered®" mantra for making healthier choices. The meme suggests humans will emerge from the pandemic in one of three states depending on their awareness, habits, and responses. She took control of her well-being and focused on "hunk."

A dear friend who was getting a bit chunky recently shared, in a hushed tone, "You know, Gayle, health isn't everything. You might want to tone things down." As a passionate certified wellness coach and personal fitness trainer, I couldn't find the words to respond; but I thought for days about her comment. Was she concerned that I might come off as an intimidating zealot? Could she benefit from gentle nudging about the fragileness of health? Not knowing that I don't judge people for their food preferences, maybe she felt self-conscious about her habits? I tried letting go of her words, but they kept rattling in my head.

Caring for Self

"Self-care is giving the world the best of you, instead of what's left of you."
— Katie Reed

Health is wealth. It's easy to take for granted, but we can't wait for health threats before we take steps to preserve it. We can't wait for a pandemic, diabetes, or other serious threat to prioritize our self-care. We must take action every day.

My passion is inspiring people so they become proactive caretakers of their health and reduce their likelihood of a dreaded wake-up call altogether. The best news? No matter where you are with your health, you can improve your self-care game (i.e., healthy eating, stress management, regular exercise) and take control of your well-being with small daily steps.

For me, the pandemic's bright spot is that many people are more aware and have stepped up their wellness efforts: lowering their risks of illness and strengthening their immunity. I hope these are lasting changes.

When we are deeply rooted in strong self-care practices, we become like trees that stand strong when a storm roars through.

"You are the sky. Everything else–it's just the weather."
— Pema Chödrön

Mindset

Mindset is like the proverbial cart and horse. We can focus on the cart (the body) to make sure it's solid. But if the horse (the mind) is untrained and lacks strength for the journey, issues with the cart are meaningless.

In addition to the happiness tenets above, four mindful, simple, and free foundations can help us become more hopeful and calm, allowing us to be a much-needed light in the world: Gratitude, laughter, attitude, and cheer.

A daily gratitude practice is an effective way to shift into a positive life view. Gratitude turns feelings of lack into abundance and enhances our ability to find silver linings, providing profound benefits with only five minutes of daily effort.

Laughter "yoga" is another powerful practice that lowers stress, strengthens immunity, and boosts moods. Laughter "clubs" are available worldwide and most are free. This weekly half-hour practice has kept me giggling for nearly ten years.

> *"Life is ninety percent attitude and ten percent action."*
> — Charles Swindoll

Everyone experiences self-doubt, tragedies, and failures. What we do with them defines us. We all get in our own way, letting negative self-talk hold us down. But we have the power to control the volume of this inner critic. When we cultivate our inner cheerleader, things have a magical way of opening up.

I've often wished for a "control-Z button" on life. There are no re-dos, but every day offers a kind of "reset" button. Everyone chooses his or her own attitude each day. You can allow negative experiences to spoil your day, week, month, or your life. Ultimately, you determine how you do *you* in life. Will you be awake and in discovery or asleep, reactive to circumstances and people? It seems that life is a constant process of nodding off and reawakening. You commit whether to be angry and resentful or to be kind and loving. The potential consequences are enormous.

Remember: You are your life's editor and have the power to craft what comes next. What will be the silver lining in your pandemic story?

My proposed amended quote:

> *"The keys to happiness are in your pocket.*
> *It's up to you to reach in every day and pull them out."*
> — Gayle Wilson Rose

Gayle Wilson Rose provides accountability, encouragement, and guidance as she assists clients in developing consistency to shift out of habits that don't support well-being and to adopt healthy mindsets for balanced self-care that lasts. With WhyPowered® Whole Health Coaching, clients say "No" to diets and "Yes" to trusting themselves and their bodies. Without relying on willpower, calorie-counting, or points, clients get to their happy weight without extremes, deprivation, or "shoulds." By connecting to their WhyPower, clients find their motivation mojo for eating cleaner, leading active lifestyles, and managing daily stressors.

With a business degree and certifications in health coaching and personal fitness training from the American Council on Exercise, Coach Gayle specializes in behavior change.

In August 2020, she published *Your Happy Weight—How To Get There and Stay There*. In 2014 she founded WhyPowered® Whole Health Coaching. Her mantra is "All things in moderation except love and laughter."

www.WhyPoweredCoaching.com
Gayle@WhyPoweredCoaching.com
www.instagram.com/whypoweredcoaching/channel/
www.facebook.com/WhyPoweredCoaching/
www.youtube.com/channel/UCJW-WrQowRKA-_SKhwOSH0A
www.linkedin.com/in/gaylerose/

Armed with Forgiveness

Nothing will get you up and out of bed faster than having your seventeen-year-old son run in and say, "I just had a gun to my head and I thought I was going to die." My husband and I could see, feel, the adrenalin running through his body as we jumped up and surged into action mode to figure out if this was a dream or reality.

It was one o'clock in the morning when he left the house to pick up his sister who had been out drinking with friends. As he stepped into the car, under poorly lit streetlights that scattered the roadside, he closed the door. What happened next would permanently change his life. As he sat there putting the coordinates into his phone, he was interrupted by the driver-side door swinging open.

He turned his head to the left to see the individual, but all he saw was the barrel of a silver-plated pistol, the pistol that could end his life—No goodbye. No last "I love you." The end. Suddenly he heard words, "Give me everything you got. Give me everything you got." With no time to react to the demand, a man reached past my son to snatch the phone in his right hand. But the phone wasn't enough for this stranger; he needed more.

Now, for my son and perhaps a majority of seventeen-year-old boys, no one is allowed to take their things—and they believe they are invisible. My son, being a well-grown and athletic young man, took a chance in the spur of the moment. He took a life-or-death chance to prove to himself that no one could touch him.

As the man tried reaching deeper into the vehicle to grab more personal belongings, my son pushed him away and made a dash for the front door. For a young man who has run up and down football fields, sprinted 200-meter dashes, and stormed around the base pads, he still is convinced that this twenty-foot run back into the house that night was the longest run of his life.

Now he won't say it too often, but there was someone else in the car with him that night. A faded two-by-two picture of Mother Mary sat on the dashboard directly behind the steering wheel. When he initially sat in the car, he saw Mary looking at him. He said verbally, "Hello."

Since my childhood, I have experienced the feeling that I am protected, but the beliefs of the Catholic church had me questioning and doubting, a lot. As I got older those beliefs brought up lots of frustrations and triggers. When I started studying metaphysics, learning breath work, exploring mediumship, and feeling more confident in my own inner guidance, I started connecting to spirits on the "other side." And you can only imagine the disbelief when Jesus and Mother Mary started appearing to me. It was in those moments I stopped doubting!! When my son said to me, "I know Mother Mary saved my life," I knew that he knew he would always be protected too. And good thing he knows that because he needs the freedom to explore life and be the risk-taker he is on Earth to be.

I think it's easy to look at any tragedy and ask questions. Why did my son live when so many others die? What is his purpose since he's still here? What are the lessons? These questions led me to have a conversation with another mom who lost her son in a similar incident a couple years earlier. As a mom, my heart hurt when I heard of this tragedy. When we met, she showed up strong. Where did that strength come from? I invited her in to have a conversation so I could ask. She explained to me that her strength came from knowing that her son left this world a hero, fearless. She was sad, yes. She missed him. But she knew without a doubt he lived.

Months and years following the encounter, my son wasn't filled with rage and hatred, but almost a feeling of grief. The kid's name was Montel; his birthday, just a few days shy of my son's birthday. He was a kid that could have played football with my son and possibly become friends with him. My son doesn't want Montel to live a life behind bars, because, although he was led down a dark path, he may never have had the intention to hurt anybody.

So, to the young man, my son says that one day he wants to talk to you, throw the football around with you, and hear your story. He would love to share his story with you.

It's really easy to live in a place of fear and anger towards someone who did harm to us. Or we can look at it all as a gift.

As a mom, this incident was my validation that we are always protected; for my son, it was his affirmation that the power of fully forgiving creates freedom. Knowing that we live in a world full of unknowns can be scary. But even the scariest times don't need to be all that scary if we stay connected to our guides on the other side, like Mary and Jesus who protect me and my family. They know the journey we are here to live.

So, ask yourself: Are there things that have happened to you that you need to forgive in order to find more freedom in your life? Do you need to forgive others? Or do you need to forgive yourself for your own actions that could be holding you back? I find the more I am steadfast in my own beliefs the more I'm naturally connected to all of those on the other side who are cheering me on to live life more like my son, fearless but ready to see the beauty in the world as it is.

Becky Schoenig is an intuitive guide. Her natural drive to question everything and listen for intuition can be traced back to elementary school where she struggled with rules and expectations that didn't make sense, all the while finding magic in little moments. Her path was spiritual from the start. The reason? Mountains can be moved when more of us stand in our power; when guilt, shame, and fear is released. Each connection made is a ripple in a larger vibration that will guide us to our purpose here on earth.

Currently, co-owner of SymBowl Restaurant in Kirkwood, Missouri, Becky uses the restaurant to connect with others in a sanctuary of fresh, flavorful whole foods. Her dream to create a table that welcomes everyone, without judgment, came true. She mentors others who desire to cut through the noise of societal expectations and trust their intuition.

www.mysymbowl.com
www.beckyschoenig.com

SOPHIE ROUMEAS

The Angel's Wings

H*is voice touched me and He said . . .*
You are rediscovering the path of Light; it could not be more grateful to Me that you harness yourself to it with intensity, faith, joy.

No one has His equal to rediscovering sacred spaces of freedom.

Your six senses activated, **it is now the turn of your body of light to be**; at the bottom of your depths is a treasure of knowledge which you will sooner or later have to bear witness so those whom you are supposed to guide can plunge towards this divine access.

Your cells have prepared over the days of your human life. But We can't wait any longer. On the ascent curve, you started to descend. Because your human spirit could not accept this internal force which is nevertheless yours.[1]

That's the problem for many of you, Humans; this upward curve descends for lack of inner resources and collective mutual aid.

The "new generation of parents" emerges, to welcome the New Children of Light.[2] Some, sent before their time as anonymous scouts, burnt sometimes their wings or could not spread them. This veil of forgetfulness which falls on the soul and the individual consciousness, by being embodied in the human vehicle, is not the easiest to lift.

We need you and all who are in the Ascension aids: This time is coming and it is no longer possible for Us to keep the truth hidden from you.

Other worlds more advanced than yours have already ascended collectively, and the correspondences of this psychomorphic field are now too heavyfor your organisms. The dissonances of this millefeuille[3] of dimensions influence your system in ways We would not have imagined happening so soon.

---

1 Kundalini force
2 Millenium children (Rainbow, Crystal, Star…)
3 yarn

The sun that warms you may one day very soon burn you because the atmospheric layer is dissolving at a faster speed than we can replenish it. **The constitution of your bodies of light must accelerate.**

The virus[4] that has already claimed so many lives is nothing compared to what awaits you in the next few years. All families of viruses and microbial strains are waking up, preparing to activate. Why? Because the garden of your humanity that has been dehumanized for so long cannot take it anymore. Synthesized seeds in clandestine laboratories will soon hatch in the open to the misfortune of our dear Mother Earth.

The roots of evil have entered our Blue Planet. The term "anchor" is no longer quite appropriate when some seek the solution to escape to other planets, before our own falls into disuse. Rediscover what "anchor" is.

You ask if there is a solution: It is written above. A mass renewal of beliefs, an army of people who facilitate the greatest number to externalize their suffering in breaths of consciousness. Only one air, on the planet, and if some countries still have the chance to breathe "clean," this evidence will soon no longer be relevant.

As many of you felt through visions, dreams, recommendations, **the earth is changing poles**. From magnetic to electric. This is not facilitating our interactions with the other planets of our galaxy. Turbulences become stronger. Earth bodies develop more and more diseases that science does not yet know how to cure when we have never been so close to returning to the level of the Golden Age of yesteryear.

The Cathedral Builders have a lot to do.[5] They try to reach the vault of heaven, whereas the foundations are not sound enough.

What do you think the soil is? **The ground for your ascension is human.** Your humanity made a vow long ago, when benevolence and Divine Love were everywhere, to rise collectively or not at all. This thinking is remembered to you today.

Collective consciousness. The sacredness of life left you a long time ago. The millions of children who have been enslaved alive, and sometimes from their tenderest years, can no longer bear this escalation of violence and contempt for them.

---

4 2020 global pandemic
5 In sacred architecture, the Cathedral is a Temple, built in the Image of the Universe like human being himself

Their hearts meet during their nights, and they share in secret their despair and suffering. Their souls sound the death knell for this indignity which rallies almost half of the population—yes, you read correctly, half of the population which takes advantage from Childhood.[6]

(End of vertical communication.)

Does this move you? Here are some recommendations:

Every day bring water to a plant, at home or in nature. **Nourish the earth with your positive intention**. It will raise the energetic vibration in and around you.

Use your senses made available by Creation. Use them to perceive the world as it is.

If you see, hear, feel someone in danger, don't ignore them. Take action, as you can, to help that person.

Remember the strength of the collective. We are not asking you to live in a community, it is already the case; your brain waves connect you all, even behind your walls; **we invite you to join forces with other people, whatever the cause**. Two people together can work miracles.

Spread your wings. Every day listen to the wisdom of your mind, body, and spirit. Specific areas connect your energetic and subtle bodies to reach and align with your higher Self.

Remember, the breeding ground of cathedrals is human. No neglect of children will be tolerated.

Rediscover the alliance of the sacred feminine and masculine, to nurture a balanced humanity where each one is respected in total integrity.

Know thyself. Many therapies work to re-establish our individual and collective divine presence.

Choose your actions. Silence helps to feel the next actions to carry out this quest for Light. Meditate when you can. Act now.

All humans who feel the calling must help themselves and their neighbors.

Each of you has the right to reach your bright spot. The Universe is designed to welcome us all. We are One.

"You cannot have wings, before you have roots."

— Francesco Di Castri

---

6 Domestic neglect, violence, trafficking, exploitation…

Sophie Roumeas is a facilitator for Change. She specializes in personal development, resilience, and activation of psychic abilities. She works with people who desire to align with their higher potential; transition between the old and the new "Me" often requires guidance and compassion.

Native of the French Alps, Sophie created **Alpes Meditation** to share a ritual of meditation for conscious living. **AM** provides classes for individuals, conscious entrepreneurs, artists, health leagues, children, and families...

Sophie tailors a unique formula with her clients, to access their inner gifts, and manifest their happiness, intuition, and innovation; coaching process is mixed à la carte with hypnosis, systemic constellation, past life regression, aura readings...

Her motto: *Let's Voice Your Soul™!*

Sophie contributed to the No. 1 International Best-Selling anthology *Step Into Your Brilliance*. She is convinced that the future of our blue-green planet resides in the balance between our individual and collective consciousness.

sophie.roumeas@gmail.com
www.sophieroumeas.com
www.alpesmeditation.com
www.mindfulcandle.com
www.facebook.com/SophieRoumeas2
www.facebook.com/pg/mindfulcandle/services
www.facebook.com/sophie.roumeas1/
www.linkedin.com/in/sophie-rouméas-33b60261
www.twitter.com/aminovation
https://m.youtube.com/channel/UC5vOTXDbgIIJVwDYHQxdqPQ

We're Going To Be Okay

As an entrepreneur and a success coach, I've helped a lot of people work through difficult things. I've also been through a lot myself. From my background, I've developed survival strategies—that usually work. But there was one moment in time when I *knew* that "we were going to be okay."

I founded a business fifteen years ago. It has had its ups and downs. But in early 2020, everything seemed to be crashing in around me; problems seemed to be stacking on top of each other. We had just recovered from a fire at our main location right before our slow, winter season. On top of everything, before we could recover, we were hit with a pandemic in March that forced us to close for an unknown amount of time.

By this point, my family and I had been in the U.S. for three years, having moved from Canada for business purposes. With four very active and involved kids, a move like that wasn't easy. Personal stress stacked on top of business stress. When the global health crisis hit, my visa was about to expire; and if immigration didn't work out soon, our plans and goals would be crushed. We would have to move back to Canada and start over.

Even if we could stay in the U.S., there was a lot to lose. I have incredible business partners, employees, and customers who have helped build our business and who rely on its success. I had personally invested everything I had into this company, financially and emotionally, over the past fifteen years. But everything seemed to be coming to a head. It wasn't good. The pandemic could push us over the edge.

Because of my past successes, I am confident in my ability to solve problems. But things were different this time. Problems were continuing to pile up, one after another; the difference was these problems were out of my control. The fire was an accident; immigration was in the hands of the government; and the pandemic was (and still is) out of anyone's control. Emotions—fear, anger, frustration, anxiety—consumed me.

As an entrepreneur, I've had to deal with these emotions before, always trying not to let them impact my family. My family is my number one priority. I have them in mind with every major decision I make. My goal in life has always been to give them incredible opportunities, experiences, and memories. But this time they could see it in me. Even if I had wanted to keep it to myself, my wife has always been able to read me; and she knew something big was wrong.

So, we sat down to talk through it. I told her everything. We discussed all possible scenarios. It weighed heavily on both of us. Then she did something that brought a complete change upon me. She stood up, looked me in the eye, and said, "We're going to be okay. I'm confident you are going to be able to figure this out. But if not and we have to face the worst, I'm with you. You and I, we're going to be okay."

It hit me like a sledgehammer. At that moment I knew that I was supported in my decisions and that she would stick with me no matter what. I knew what I needed to do and my confidence to do it, with my wife by my side, had just grown.

Our lives are shaped by our decisions. And with so much happening earlier this year that was out of my control, my process for decision-making wouldn't guarantee success; but it would allow me to have clarity, to make better decisions, and deal with outcomes.

The following strategies helped me, and maybe will help you, make the best decisions possible:

1. **Find clarity.** To achieve anything, we have to focus and be clear on what we want and why we want it. Focusing on what we don't want, won't get us closer to our desired outcome. When I focused on what I didn't want, I felt fear, anger, frustration, and anxiety. Ultimately, I found it important to focus on two things: (1) what I could control and (2) what mattered most. I couldn't change what was out of my

control, so I focused my energy on things I could control and what I wanted for those who mattered the most.

2. **Be proactive.** With clarity, we can discover possible solutions. After I had clarity, I moved, proactively, toward what I wanted, which changed the impact that fear was having on me so that I could make the best decisions for my family and me. Why give fear control and power over our decisions? Fear is not useful and when we overcome it, we will see and move toward better decisions.

3. **Build a support group.** We are always going to face difficult things in life. When we surround ourselves with people who will support, encourage, and help us, those tough times are more manageable. A support system helps us to get through the difficulties and make our best decisions. I am fortunate that I have always had this type of support from my wife; it has helped me through some strenuous times.

* * *

This process didn't make all my problems go away. Today, I'm still dealing with some of the issues. Although our move to the U.S. at one time looked unrealistic (immigration took longer than we expected), it eventually worked out. We are now settled and established in our new home in Arizona.

My decision-making process helped me to clarify what I wanted and enabled me to be proactive getting there. It helped me to recognize and accept what I can and cannot control so that I could funnel my energy to the right things. Finally, my support group helped me to keep the things that matter most to me at the center of my decisions.

And without a doubt, "We're going to be okay!"

Jeff Heggie is an entrepreneur and success coach with a passion for helping others achieve their biggest dreams. As a coach, Jeff starts with a focus on mindset. Taking his client or their business to the next level always begins with the right mindset.

Jeff enjoys using his extensive experience in the banking industry, over twenty years as an entrepreneur, plus his training and experience as a coach to help his clients break through the mental and physical barriers that hold them back.

Jeff and his wife, Tamara, both grew up in Southern Alberta but now make Arizona home. Family and sports have always been important to him. He loves spending time coaching or watching his kids. He's a former professional rodeo cowboy and has over twenty years' experience coaching basketball.

www.jeffheggie.com
jeff@jeffheggie.com
https://beacons.ai/jeffheggiecoaching
www.instagram.com/jeffheggiecoaching/
www.linkedin.com/in/jeffheggie/
www.facebook.com/JeffHeggieCoaching

SANDY BARTLETT

Being Mindfully Confident

How many times do you get knocked down before you quit fighting back? I'm not talking about physically getting knocked down; that would be a different story. I'm referring to those things that strike you to the core. Those things that make your confidence falter. What is it that makes some get up and others give up? I've certainly had my share of knockdowns—too many to share in this one chapter.

I don't know why some get up and fight and some don't. However, what I do know is that you are worthy! Don't ever let anyone tell you that you're not.

I worked with a client who struggled with this. She has had a hard time putting herself first her entire life. Recently, she shared with me how someone had blasted her on the phone. I was so proud when she shared with me that she had stood up for herself and told this individual that the manner in which she was being spoken to was unacceptable and she would not accept it—from the caller or anyone else. Bravo!

Eleanor Roosevelt once said, "No one has the right to make you feel inferior without your consent." I love this quote. Are you giving anyone permission to make you feel inferior? When is the last time you thought about this? Do you need to give yourself permission to stand up for you?

As I write this I am at home, confined to my room, recovering from the illness striking many others throughout the globe. Fortunately, my symptoms are on the mild side. You see, I tend to be "a glass half full" kind of gal; I choose to find the positive. I choose not to focus on the negative. So while I take "laps" in my bedroom to get some movement in, I repeat out loud to myself and the universe, "I am healthy. I am strong. My lungs are clear. I will beat this." Why do

I do this? It's called "Mindful Confidence," and I lead an entire group on Facebook dedicated to this topic.

Let me paint a picture for you:

Do you struggle with how to say what you need? Or do you have it all played out in your mind what someone's reaction will be? Do you feel like you are in the game alone without support? Do you expect others to "know" what you need before you say it? Finally, do you struggle with how to say "no" to anyone?

Putting everyone else first can be our greatest quality, but it can also be our biggest flaw. You see, I believe we cannot pour from an empty cup. If we aren't taking care of ourselves, how can we take care of others?

So how do we change this? First, take stock of the big five areas of your life—physical, mental, relationships, financial, and "That Which is Greater." Evaluate each one. Picture these items as spokes in a wheel. Picture a dot on each spoke to represent how well you feel about that area of your life. The closer to the outside the wheel your dot is, the better you are doing in that area. Is your wheel perfectly round? Or does it clatter down the street like you are on cobblestone?

Now, pick the one area you'd like to work on first. What is most important to you? In a perfect world, you wave a magic wand and say to yourself, "I can achieve _____." Then ask yourself, "When less-than-perfect happens, I can achieve _____." You see, it's about mindset. Sometimes you just need to pivot and reframe. Here is a simple example: In a perfect world, I will say affirmations every day. When less-than-perfect happens, I, at least, will say my affirmations on the weekends. Not perfect, but I give myself permission to do a little less rather than not at all.

MY TIPS:

Learn to love the sound of your feet walking away from things not meant for you. It's okay. Recognize all the things you don't want in life, reframe them, and begin to create new things. Be willing to take imperfect action. Be messy—that's how we learn. It doesn't matter how small the step. What matters is that you take it.

Give yourself permission. I worked with a client recently who struggled a couple of weeks each month with energy. We landed on her creating two lists—one was a high-energy activity list and one was a low-energy activity list. It was about giving herself permission to do activities on the low-energy days. She had it in her the entire time; she just needed to give herself permission to be okay with it.

Forgive. Guilt and resentment are destructive emotions. Forgiveness will cause everything to grow. And don't forget to forgive yourself while you're at it.

Stop apologizing. Especially for things that are not your responsibility. One of my favorite sayings is, "The only thing you can control is your response to things." So, quit taking responsibility for things out of your control. It is not your job to solve everyone else's problems. Yes, it will take practice. And I promise you, the more you do it, the easier it will become. Stretch those muscles. And don't beat yourself up if it doesn't work each time. Forgive yourself and try again next time.

Stop postponing feeling good. Make a running list of simple things that you know make you feel good. Pick something on that list and do it daily.

If you can't get something done today, there is always tomorrow. I learned this lesson a long time ago. I would work long hours and then take work home that I never touched. And you know what I learned? No one cared. I learned that it's the deadlines that matter. As long as I was meeting deadlines, I was in good shape.

So remember: You are worthy! Practice being mindful. I believe in you. Believe in yourself!

Sandy Bartlett maintains a dual certification as a life/health coach and is currently working on a mastery level certification in Transformational Coaching Method. She helps women find their voices in asking for what they need. She has coordinated retreats and support groups for women in leadership. With a proven record of success, Sandy makes a difference in the lives of others through the power of empathy and the influence of support.

Sandy holds a master's degree in human resources management and has over thirty years' experience in human resources. Her focus on people and education provides valuable insight into employee relations, benefits, and risk management.

Sandy and her husband make a home in Bullhead City, Arizona.

www.thesandybartett.com
www.daocloud.com/pro/sandy-bartlett
hello@thesandybartlett.com
www.linkedin.com/in/thesandybartlett/
www.twitter.com/sandybartlett56
www.facebook.com/groups/mindfulconfidenceforwomen
www.instagram.com/thesandybartlett/

MARCI D. TOLER

The Before and the After

There are markers of time. The before and the after.
Some are joyous markers...
the first kiss, the sunrise, the birth of a child.

Some are hard markers...
the first morning alone, the death of a child, the dark night of the soul.

There are markers of time. The before and the after.

The before the war, the after the war.
The before he left, the after he left.
The before the dream was shattered and the after.

This is the story of the pause. It isn't pretty. It isn't tied up with a bow.
There is no happy ending...yet.
There is only the story of the pause. And the hope of what is to come.
It's a story of survival, of resilience, of despair, of hope. Of high moments and the return to the low, dark places, only to come again to the place of hope and peace. It's a story of sorrow and regret, a story of restoration and hope.
It's my story. And it may hold pieces of your story and your healing.

There is a certain naiveté that comes before "the after." A certain curtain that separates you from even the possibility of life after an event. And the odd thing of our commonality is that the "Dark Night of the Soul" event is so individualized that what is mine is not yours. What is a life-altering, forever life-shifting event for one, is just a road bump for another.

My story is a series of what I considered road bumps, potential life-altering, forever life-shifting events; but in my naiveté, I arrogantly assumed I was above it all. I would rise again. It would not define me. These were just moments in time, events to overcome.

The death of one parent,

and then the other,

the death of a child,

sending a spouse to war,

deploying to war myself,

the end of a career,

the end of a marriage. These would not define me. And they haven't.

But what has defined me is…well, me!

I used titles to define me. (Oh, don't read this and think you are above that.) I am a daughter, a sister, a cousin. I am a college student, a business major. I am an Army officer. I am a wife, a mother. I have three, no two, no three children. I am an ex-wife. I am a retired Army officer. I am an Army spouse. A combat veteran. An author. A leader. A follower. A partner. The list goes on and on.

In many of those roles, I understood who I wanted to be in the role. I understood the rules and expectations, so I knew how to be successful in that role. Some I grew into; some I grew out of. Some I left behind.

But in the after…I don't know the rules. I don't know who is expecting what? Who am I expecting to be?

And in that pause, between the before and the after…there is no belonging, and with no belonging there is a loss of who I've always been. But, in that pause there is a glimpse of the opportunity to be who I always wanted to be. To be the me I've always known myself to be.

It is a faint glimmer of hope, a quickening of my heart, not quite an image in my mind's-eye of who I was destined to be. But it leaves in its wake the hope of what can be. If only I can see it. If only I can open myself up to the journey of possibilities.

If only I can learn to dream again.

If only I can learn to trust myself again.

That seems too far. Too hard. Look at the past. Who am I? I fell, I failed, I broke relationships, I hurt and was hurt. I was not trustworthy and not trusting. Who am I?

But again and again the glimmer of hope returns. Again and again, the door labeled "trust" closes. I cry. I pout. I search. I hope. I pray. I pound on the door. I seek. I ignore.

I wait. I grow. I heal.

And now it's time.

I stand with my hand on the door labeled "trust." I take a deep breath, close my eyes, and open the door. The sparkle of the glimmer calls to me. I reach my hand to grasp, to hold on, and it escapes. It calls me forward, and I reach, not wanting to let go. The door, it grounds me. I know that place. I know I can close it and retreat. I know that place, in the pause.

The glimmer sparkles and shines. I feel my soul reaching forward to meet the sparkle, and I see them dance. My heart beating so loudly I can't hear the music. My mind reacting, searching for the place it knows.

And I know I must choose. My after is waiting.

My soul calls my mind to remember. It knows what courage is.

My soul calls my heart to remember we are not alone.

My soul calls my feet to dance.

And I'm left with the choice. I choose to dance.

Marci D. Toler (Lt. Col. Ret., US Army) is the founder and senior project manager of Marci & Company. She is a marketing and business analyst, mentor, author, and speaker. She combines strategic thinking, marketing and process improvement, and leader and/or team development to support leaders and organizations to stand out from the crowd and have a deep impact in the world. Marci holds a bachelor's degree from Colorado State University in business economics and econometrics. She went on to earn her Master of Business Administration in Change Management and was selected for and graduated from the United States Senior Service College (US Army War College) with a Master of Strategic Studies.

During her thirty-three years of service in the US Army, she served in several combat zones and received multiple honors including the Bronze Star, multiple Meritorious Service Medals, Army Commendation Medals, Army Achievement Medals, and two Meritorious Unit Commendation awards.

Marci can be reached at www.marciandcompany.com

DR. DAVID ALEXANDER

Bright Spots in a World of Awakening Social Responsibility

Everyone has an image of what success and happiness or the "good life" looks like for them. Most people want the same basic things: a place to call home, loved ones to share it with, enough food to eat, and the financial resources to enjoy life. Like many Americans, my "dream life" centered around owning my own home and starting a family.

In 2013 that dream life was coming into shape. I met my forever love and I knew that every past experience had prepared me for this! Two years later we began in earnest to plan for the expansion of our family. She already had a son— he was nine when we met—but we both wanted to add a child, buy a house, and have that "good life." Seems pretty straight forward, doesn't it? The all-American dream. Well, there are a few additional things you should know that add valuable context.

First and foremost, my now wife and her first born son are from Zambia. Now, you might wonder, why should that matter. For starters it was only fifty years ago that *Loving v. Virginia*[1]—a landmark Supreme Court case—legally protected "interracial" marriage. The second reason is that raising an African American boy in the climate of Travon Martin, Tamir Rice, Michael Brown, et cetera, is different than any other parenting task and ought not be considered lightly by a privileged white man such as myself. I considered this aspect when dating my wife. I knew then that stepping forward into a serious relationship would bring challenges and unique burdens that I would have to carry for a lifetime. Ones for which I may

---

1 Loving v. Virginia. 388 US 1 (US Supreme Court 1967)

not feel adequately prepared, educated, or equipped to handle. And while I recognize that all parents feel some sort of ill-equippedness, this was by all accounts a wholly different realm.

Our love continued to grow and our vision for our dream life continued to flourish.

In 2015, when the housing market was hot, we had the opportunity to purchase a home well under market value. How did we end up with such a sweet deal? Well, it was a house that had not been lived in for two years but was still "maintained" by the owner who lived out of state. So we made an offer to do the heavy lifting of cleaning the property up (inside and out), leasing for a year and building our down payment into the monthly lease. This was a huge win-win! The owner would get out of the mortgage, and we would get our starter home to build our family. Besides, who is afraid of a little hard work, especially in your first home? It was a dream come true, and just in time. My partner was pregnant!

So feeling blessed with opportunity and filled with optimism, we move in and got to work. We painted, redid floors, cleaned, excavated, and continued to dream. The next chapter of our dream includes having our wedding in the backyard. And boy, did we need to have vision in order to even consider it. You see, at the time of moving in, our very large backyard—which wrapped around the property and included fruit trees and raised garden beds—was hidden under a sea of five-foot blackberry bushes. In the great Pacific Northwest, blackberry bushes grow like weeds. They are invasive and relentless. Cutting them back or mowing them down only helps to produce more. They must be removed by the roots—which are six to twelve inches underground.

So I got to work, cutting, piling, digging, and removing blackberry bushes every weekend and spare moment I had. The problem was, they kept growing back, seemingly faster than I could dig them up. So I did double time, morning shifts, evening shifts, in between meetings at work. Nothing less than the removal of every single root or piece of root would do. I was at it for months; there was no end in sight. One particular spring afternoon, I came home after a five-day business trip. I was crushed when I entered the backyard. To my eyes it looked as if I had made little or no progress at all. With a heavy sigh, I picked up a hoe (my third one, having broken the others) and got back to work.

On April 19, 2015, Freddie Gray, a twenty-five-year-old black man, died in police custody after excessive use of force and a mishandling of his safe transport. Sick with grief, I took out my anger and frustration on the ground that contained unnumbered blackberry roots. Grief, because it was another senseless death, another piece of evidence that says black lives do not matter in our society. I was struck with the pain and anguish that this was the world that I was bringing another black body into. Another black male. Soon I would be the father of not only my wife's first born, but my first born. I would be responsible for raising these young men in a world that seeks to harm, judge, and punish them because of the color of their skin. I cried and pounded the ground with my garden hoe, tearing at the earth, a feverish, desperate attempt to rip the roots from their embedded place of trespass.

The blackberry roots had become a metaphor for the embedded and entrenched racism that was choking life from my (our) American dream. My grief turned to rage as I appealed to the heavens, "This is not my fault! I did not plant these bushes!" Then in my exhausted state, leaning on my garden hoe, I heard a voice, "Yes, but it is your land now."

The roots of racism run deep in our country, and many of us may feel exhausted by the amount of heavy lifting or even think, "It's not our fault." Yet the greater truth is, it's our land now.

Rev. Dr. David Alexander currently serves as the spiritual director for Spiritual Living Center of Atlanta. Previously, he pastored New Thought Center for Spiritual Living in Lake Oswego, Oregon, for fifteen years. A social justice activist, Dr. David has served on the Board of Directors for the Community of Welcoming Congregations, a Portland-based alliance which provides "a voice for LGBTQ and allied people of faith."

A student of New Thought history and philosophy, Dr. David writes a monthly column for Science of Mind magazine and received an honorary Doctor of Divinity degree from the Centers for Spiritual Living (CSL) in 2014.

In 2015, Dr. David was inducted into the College of Bishops and Affirming Faith Leaders by the Fellowship of Affirming Ministries. In 2016, he was recognized with a Force for Good Award from Unity of Sacramento.

David lives in Lawrenceville, Georgia, with his wife, Patience, their two sons, and their dog, Cooper.

RevDrDavidAlexander@slc-atlanta.org
www.revdavidalexander.com
www.slca.com
www.facebook.com/NamasteDave

SARAH VICTORY

The Magic of Possibilities

Imagine you're standing on a stage, looking at nearly two thousand people. You've spoken to over a thousand groups, so you're feeling surprisingly confident. You ask your favorite question: "If you could do magic, what would you *really* want for your future?" Everyone is sharing their bravest ideas with a partner. The room is buzzing with excitement and enthusiasm.

You feel a bit like a rock star. You're sure you just grew a few inches taller.

Suddenly, you notice a man up the center aisle. He does not look happy at all. He stands and he's big, very big, with wild hair and an angry gleam in his eye.

He marches down the aisle, storms up on the stage, and towers over you.

Well, this is exactly what was happening to me. I'm not a big woman; I'm barely five foot four, so this guy scares me.

I think, *Any nice bouncers in this place, who could take care of this guy?*

He glowers down at me, "Little lady, you can't tell people they can just have anything they want! There's a lot of things I'll never have."

"Uh…" *Why has no one noticed my potential loss of life here?*

The man's tag says, "Edward."

"Edward, you seem pretty upset. I can understand that; it's hard to want things that you feel you'll never have. So, I'll make a deal with you. You let me spend the next forty-five minutes telling these people they can have whatever they want, giving some suggestions on how they can get those things, and after that, we can talk about what I could do differently and what it is that you really want. If that doesn't work, you can always kill me later."

Edward cracks a small smile, or possibly a sneer, but it's a start.

Later on… "Edward, could you tell me what you feel you'll never have?"

Edward's face hardens. "I want a yacht. They are very expensive and I'm a teacher. I teach in the inner city. Those kids need me. You telling us we can have 'anything' is total BS."

"So, a yacht would mean a lot to you. How come?"

"I've always loved boats, yachts especially. They're beautiful on the water. I used to help repair them as a teenager. I got good at it too."

"I have a crazy idea for you. Isn't there a yacht club near you?"

"Yes."

"Then go there and talk to people. Ask their opinions about yachts."

Edward has now decided I'm nuts but he reluctantly says, "Okay."

Two weeks later, my phone rings.

"Little lady!"

"Edward?"

"I'm coming over!"

Thirty minutes later I am surrounded by my entire staff, just in case, and Edward walks in. He throws his arms around me, picking me up off my feet.

"You won't believe it!"

He shares that he went to the yacht club. He asked a lot of questions and the answers were fascinating. He immediately made friends who were as passionate about yachts as he was.

Seeing his enthusiasm, an elderly couple from Canada came to talk to him. Now, they were both about 108 years old, but their passion for yachts and people was obvious. They also shared a love of children and education.

They say, "We sure wish we could find someone like you!"

"What?" Edward responds.

"We love our yacht like it is our baby and lately it's been a struggle."

"Why is that?"

"Well, now, there's been vandalism and repairs needed that we didn't know about, leading to serious damage. You see, we come down here for couple of months in the winter and then couple of months in the summer, so we're not here to keep an eye on it. With getting older, it's getting harder to do too. So, we've been looking everywhere for someone to yacht sit."

Edward's jaw drops. "Yacht sit? That's a thing?"

"Sure is, eh." (They ARE Canadian). "Can't find anyone 'cause all the good folks like you already have a yacht."

"But I don't have a yacht," stammers Edward.

"Then you're an answer to a prayer!" say the now-grinning Canadians.

"I am good at fixing things, especially yachts. I'd love to help."

"Wonderful! We'd be happy to put you up when we are here, or we could fly you north, so you could stay at our home in British Columbia." (A home, he would later discover would more likely be referred to as a "mansion.")

Edward goes on to tell me that he was floored. Never in his whole life has anything like this ever happened.

Several years later, I was invited to a party Edward had on the yacht. After a couple of hours of touring, he told us about how much he loved taking his young students out for rides on the yacht. The Canadians were there, and they said it gave them a whole new lease on life seeing these happy young people with so much promise ahead of them.

Edward tells the teens that even though they live in the inner city, anything is possible for them, as long as they continue to work hard and believe in the beauty of their dreams. He asks them, "If you could do magic, what would you *really* want for your future?"

He tells them, "You have to believe in the magic of possibilities."

Edward reminds us of the importance of believing in others and believing in ourselves. There are always more ways to accomplish your dreams than any of us can even conceive of, and we all can be guided by the *magic of possibilities.*

(The latest news on Edward: You remember those Canadians? Well, it turns out they didn't have any children or heirs. Since they have fallen in love with Edward, can you guess who gets the yacht and plenty of money for upkeep in their will? Yep, Edward. Eventually, your dreams that matter most can come true if you believe in a little magic.)

Sarah Victory is the author of numerous books and audio programs including two best sellers, *Double Your Business in One Year or Less!* and *Do Something Brave Every Day.*

Sarah has spoken for over 1000 distinguished audiences in Europe, the US and South America.

Sarah has also been on TV, radio and newspapers coast to coast reaching over 3.5 million people!

Her clients include Avon, Ford, Redken, Farmers Insurance, Mary Kay, Oxford, Usana, OPI, Arbonne, and IBM just to name a few!

A trusted coach and business consultant, Sarah has worked with over 500 influential individual clients in the last 23 years. You have seen her clients in dozens of appearances on Oprah, *the Today Show, the Tonight Show,* and *CNN.*

Sarah's latest popular book is called *How to Be Powerful"* and is available on Amazon!

www.thevictorycompany.com
www.linkedin.com/in/sarahvictory
www.facebook.com/sarahvictory
https://www.instagram.com/realsarahvictory/

EILEEN OTERO WOLFINGTON

Finding Your Bright Spot After Loss

Have you ever experienced a loss so profound that when you hit rock bottom, you felt that you would NEVER heal? Did well-intentioned family members, friends, or colleagues say any of the following: *"When one door closes, another door opens"* (loss of a job); *"I wish you were back to being your old self"* (loss due to a divorce); *"There's light at the end of the tunnel"* (loss of a home); *"It will get better soon"* (loss of a loved one). Perhaps you have already read numerous self-help books, viewed various YouTube videos, Googled countless credible websites, talked to therapists, attended a support group, or maybe you did nothing at all. Know that these are all choices and that whatever choice you selected, it was the appropriate decision for you during that moment.

Would you believe me if I told you that the potential to navigate through those blurry dark clouds amidst all the emotional chaos can exist for you? Let me tell you why I believe that you have the innate ability to find your bright spot after a loss.

Six years ago, my father was diagnosed with the early stages of prostate cancer. Being in his early eighties, it was not recommended that he have his prostate removed. He managed living with this diagnosis for five years while receiving monthly injections and monitoring his PSA levels. In 2020, his PSA levels began to rise. As with many cancer diagnoses, radiation treatment was recommended. Having worked as a community health worker for five years within a clinic, it was not uncommon for me to research chronic diseases or ask medical providers what is the worst that could happen. So, I asked the question. "Doctor, in your years of experience, what is the potential prognosis of someone my father's age given his current PSA levels?" He replied, "While radiation treatment may help some, if he elects to not have any treatment, I would give him six months to one year." In case you're wondering, yes, Dad was in the exam room and, yes, he heard what the doctor said. Though I broached the subject, this was not something that was brought up again. While some may call this denial, neither death nor final wishes were ever discussed. In fact, Dad often said, "I'm going to live to be one hundred years old." Dad lived an abundant and zestful life.

I moved in with him on Valentine's Day to be his primary caregiver when the decision was made to bring in hospice care. He took his last breath on April 28, 2020, at age eighty-seven.

> *"After his death, I began to see him as he had really been.*
> *It was less like losing someone than discovering someone."*
>
> — Nancy Halle

As you've no doubt discovered, the loss I've decided to focus on in this chapter is the physical loss of a loved one. Allow me to share the nuggets of knowledge that I collected during my journey. Exploring these options may help you to minimize avoidance when facing loss.

Nuggets of knowledge

1. If someone you love is diagnosed with a terminal illness, learn as much as you can about end-of-life. The more you know about early signs and symptoms, the more it may help to lessen a lot of the fear that you have. You, a family member, or caregiver might even consider attending End-of-Life Doula training. You would be amazed at how beautiful the end of life can be for your loved one and your family, for example, as you plan a vigil or a legacy project.

2. Explore both palliative care and hospice care to see if the services they provide would be beneficial both to your loved one and to your family. Not only do they provide pain management, but they also assign a team that will support you. This may consist of a nurse, a social worker, a chaplain, a certified nursing assistant, and a grief counselor.

3. Consider expanding your horizon by finding your inner strength, by learning how to meditate, or listening to guided imagery. Start a self-care

regime to reduce and manage the stress you will have when caring for a loved one, especially if you are working full time and caring for your own family. Listening to positive affirmations or any type of healing music might also help.

4. Read as much as you can about death, dying, and near-death experiences. When you begin to learn with an open mind how dying individuals feel an overwhelming sense of calmness, perhaps you, too, will also feel their calm.

5. Whatever religion you practice or whatever beliefs you have, try to learn how death is viewed and understood. The more you understand the more you can calm your fear of death and dying.

6. Remember, it is okay to grieve, to cry, to mourn, to get angry, to shout, et cetera. Allow yourself to release all your emotions. However, if these remain excessive and ongoing, then it may be time for you to seek professional help.

We are living during a time of uncertainty. It is critical for you to take time to reflect on the things that are important to you. You are resilient. You have a solid foundation to make the appropriate decisions for yourself and your loved one during this time.

I've shared the most sorrowful yet most rewarding experience in my life with you today. Is loss painful? Of course it is. Can you be reconciled with your loss? The choice is up to you. May any fear and anxiety that you have felt toward loss in the past or feel today or may feel in the future be replaced with love, understanding, forgiveness, and acceptance.

In ending, I'd like to encourage you to attend a Death Cafe. Discussing mortality doesn't have to be morbid. It happens to all of us.

"Walking with a friend in the dark
is better than walking alone in the light."

— Helen Keller

Eileen Otero Wolfington is the bilingual health and wellness program coordinator for a nonprofit organization, LifeWise StL, in the city of St. Louis. For the previous five years, she was a community health worker at a local nonprofit clinic. Promoting disease prevention and healthy food choices inspired her passion to motivate low-income adult immigrant and minority women to begin a path toward wellness.

Eileen is currently studying to become a certified healing-touch practitioner to provide an alternative form of medicine that promotes stress reduction and relaxation to the mind, body, and spirit. Her sessions can include an Aroma-Touch® technique to lessen tension. She recently completed End-of-Life Doula training and is exploring becoming a grief counselor. She's a Zumba instructor who also enjoys sharing her Mexican and Puerto Rican folkloric dance in the community.

Eileen has a bachelor's degree in General Business and a master's degree in Adult Education.

SelfCareWithEileen@gmail.com
www.linkedin.com/in/eileen-wolfington-033334135/
www.facebook.com/eileen.wolfington
www.inpowerinstitute.com/team/eileen-wolfington/

CINDY ROWAN

"Life's Unfinished Business"

Perhaps it's an unrealized goal, a project never started or stalled, or just something that we might be inclined to note with a capital "I" for incomplete: unfinished business. My own encounter with unfinished business yielded some unexpected life lessons that came as a byproduct of that experience.

There I sat at my cousin's graduation. She was getting her doctorate from the same university and program that I had attended and then left twenty years ago. The realization that I had not completed my degree was inescapable. I'd come face to face with a major piece of my life's unfinished business! My mind drifted: from my high school guidance counselor telling me to not waste money going to college (I enjoyed the social aspects of school much more than the academics!), to how I became the late bloomer who found a passion to learn despite things not coming with ease, to the sacrifices of time, resources, and relationships, to juggling life while completing course requirements and getting halfway through the dissertation process before walking away.

When that goal became my unfinished business, I was in the midst of divorce, my father had suddenly passed away, and my career path felt uncertain. Stressed and overwhelmed, I was sitting in a feedback session with some members of my dissertation committee. As we engaged in what felt like a debate over whether the word should be "among" or "between" in my paper, I checked out. Enough! I didn't need this. Obviously, this encounter was the straw that broke the proverbial camel's back. I was worn out. I felt like my best wasn't good enough and every self-doubt I ever had hit me square in the face. I believed I needed to put my doctoral dissertation on the back burner.

Twenty years passed. I had done well in my career. I'd changed professions, so the degree wasn't a necessity, but the title of "doctor" was indeed my piece of unfinished business. In the academic world, the label for my status was "ABD" (All But Dissertation). That term felt worse than "Incomplete"! Of course, people asked if I'd finished and I would make up some plausible response. But it was always there, even if buried away with all of the justifications in my mind.

My cousin's graduation made me realize that maybe it was time to complete my unfinished business: write the dissertation and finish my doctorate. I arranged a meeting with the university faculty to discuss what I might have to do. They were unsure of how to proceed with me after I had been away so long. They challenged my relevance and commitment. That challenge made me realize that this was indeed what I *wanted* to do, but I was petrified of whether I *could* do it! The faculty and I agreed on a plan that would not be easy, but I needed to commit because this was my last shot at finishing.

I was thrust into a dissertation seminar group with colleagues much younger and much more technologically savvy. I felt old and inadequate. Once I engaged more with the group, though, I realized that they too had their feelings of inadequacy! Ironically, they were intrigued by my background and desire to finish. We shared our strengths and challenges with each other, which made conversations rich, relationships supportive, and the process less daunting.

While there were a few stumbling blocks on the journey to finishing, I took them in stride. I didn't have to be perfect; I just had to do my best and surrender to a system I couldn't control. I drew on my strengths, acknowledged my challenges, and sought help from others (which was not comfortable for me). Three years upon re-entry, my research was complete and my dissertation written, but was I really "finished"? I still had to complete my defense. At that moment I realized the whole process was so much more than just attaining a degree. I reflected on the rich life lessons I'd learned, namely:

- **Accept that unfinished business is often a choice.** Sometimes we make ourselves the angry victim of circumstance, but is that realistic? Our choices, particularly procrastination, which blocks our ability to move forward, are self-imposed. I've learned, if something is too big or overwhelming, to break it down into smaller pieces and don't make something bigger than it is. It's not all or nothing.

- **Build on Strengths.** In relation to my strengths, there were areas that I needed to develop to get up to speed after twenty years. I tried not to view them as *weaknesses* or beat myself up. I embraced areas for development as opportunities to learn something new or to become more proficient.

- **Get out of Your Own Way.** Asking for help and support from others was not my nature. I thought I needed to do it all myself. But how rich the learning experience became when I was open to others. Again, not a weakness, but rather a strengthening from relationships on the road to completion.

- **Unfinished business isn't a failure.** It's an incomplete. It's better to address and challenge the real reasons for incompleteness and then commit to a course of action. Fear of failure may loom, but what's the alternative? Sometimes completing unfinished business may not be achievable. Unfeasibility needs to be challenged, but then, if necessary, we need to accept it and move on.

The final requirement to attain my degree was my dissertation defense. After my two-hour defense, I waited with anticipation as my committee met behind closed doors to discuss my fate. Had I finished or would there be more to complete?

Then the door opened wide. My committee stood. And with a warm smile, my mentor said, "**DOCTOR** Rowan, we'd like you to join us back in the room." The tears flowed. The weight was lifted, and I was indeed finished!

Looking back, completing this piece of unfinished business was one of the brightest spots on my journey.

Dr. Cindy Rowan serves as president of Performance Management Solutions, a consulting firm she established in 1992. Her firm helps organizations improve profitability through organizational and talent development. Dr. Rowan's expertise in designing and implementing initiatives in the areas of leadership and management excellence, creation of coaching cultures, and performance management has yielded significant growth to the clients that she serves.

As an adjunct professor, Dr. Rowan instructs graduate level courses in human resource training and development, as well as organizational behavior and development. Her specialized firm, Performance Management Solutions for Higher Education, is dedicated to assisting colleges and universities in developing cultures of service excellence and leaders at all levels.

Dr. Rowan has received numerous honors for her work and has made presentations at local, national, and international conferences on topics related to training, leadership development, and mentoring. Her doctoral degree is from Seton Hall University in New Jersey.

perfms@aol.com
www.perfms.com
www.facebook.com/Performance-Management-Solutions-102326731579668/?ref=page_internal
www.linkedin.com/in/cynthia-rowan-44a15712/
www.twitter.com/PerfmsRowan

KEVIN HANCOCK

Staying on Mission in a Chaotic World

In the first decades of the twenty-first century, three exceptional yet unforeseen events shocked, then altered, humanity's course.

On the morning of September 11, 2001, a small group of al-Qaeda militants hijacked four airplanes. Within hours thousands would be dead, two trade towers would fall, and a global war on terror would commence. In 2008, subprime borrowers began defaulting on their home mortgages, initiating a financial crisis that nearly collapsed the entire banking system of the United States. In late 2019, a small group of shoppers at a food market in Wuhan, China, became infected with a virus of unknown origins. Within a hundred days, nearly every nation on earth was paralyzed under the weight of lock-downs and quarantines. Along the way political leaders fought to assign blame while the media empire streamed headlines and commentary. Citizens joined the fray, taking to their social media platforms to post opinions and debate.

In such times of epic social disruptions, how do we stay focused on our personal mission and voice? How do we stay educated and compassionate with regard to the crisis du jour while also remaining calm, centered, and productive with respect to our individual aspirations? How do we support the whole while advancing our sense of self?

Maintaining one's personal energy in a sea of social chaos may be the essential skill of our time.

Every voice is unique by design. The long arch of humanity is a collective journey, but that odyssey is ultimately the sum of its individual parts. What society needs most from you is for you to stay the course in pursuit of your never-to-be-repeated path and voice.

I was sensitized to the importance of authentic voice and personal mission by yet another combination of unexpected events. In 2010, I began to have trouble speaking. I was CEO of one of America's oldest family businesses and our lumber company was reeling from the stress of the economic crisis when my voice failed me. Months later I was diagnosed with a rare neurological disorder called "spasmodic dysphonia" (SD). Suddenly, I had to develop a new strategy for leading that did not include lots of talking.

Two years later, I began traveling from Maine to the remote Pine Ridge Indian Reservation in South Dakota (a place I have now been over twenty times). There I encountered an entire community that did not feel fully heard. These two events combined to produce a series of personal learnings. First, I understood what it was like to not feel fully heard. Second, I realized there were lots of ways for people to lose their voice in this world. Third, I wondered if the very purpose of a human life on earth was to self-actualize. Perhaps we were all here just trying to find our own true voice. But unfortunately, across centuries, many leaders had done more to restrict the voices of others than to liberate them. That's when my personal calling became clear. The partial loss of my own voice was an invitation to dispersed power, shared leadership, and strengthened voices of others. I have stayed focused on this mission ever since despite the temptations for distraction that the larger world affords.

To meet the challenge of remaining on course during a time of chaos takes intentionality. First, I must recognize that my own work, passions, and voice are important and worthy of refinement and advancement. Second, I need to compartmentalize what is happening around me. Aware yes. Consumed no. Finally, I need the courage to look inward and the fortitude to hold my own personal energy. The news and social discourse shall not determine my mood or control my agenda. As for the larger change we wish to see in the world? The trick, as Gandhi suggested, is to become it.

Influencing the world is an inside job. When the energy of the collective overtakes us, we lose our unique ability to contribute to humanity's advancement. You have a mission and that mission matters. Only you can pursue it. Humanity needs you to be you and carry on. With this approach in mind, the world morphs into a different place. It slows down, gains clarity, and localizes.

All three history-altering events described herein share a root cause: The human race is moving too fast. Our pace, or you might even call it our "race," is unsustainable, and it has been for quite some time. In our historic zeal to conquer and colonize the globe lives the underpinning of radical Islamic instability and terror. The subprime mortgage market collapse was also the result of impatience and excess. A decade earlier, President Clinton decided that homeownership should be expanded. There were multiple potential strategies but we chose the short-cut by lowering the borrowing standards. Excessive speed was also at work with the global pandemic. For decades airlines had been packing people into tighter and tighter spaces. How many customers can we cram onto a cruise ship, into a stadium, or inside a subway car? Humans everywhere played along and so we raced to see more and do more. How many tasks could be accomplished in a day? How many meetings could be held? Bigger, better, more—go, go, go. We all drank the Kool-Aid, joined the race, and played along. And here we are…

Once we recognize the cause of our chaos, we can hone in on the cure. The world, as seen on TV, manifests as overwhelming. Only by returning to what lies within us can we clear the skies. We each also have a solemn oath to propel and compel the spirit within us to dance in a space-time continuum reserved for you alone. Staying on your mission is the remedy to the chaos that plagues our modern world. So for the love of humanity, follow your voice. Walk your path. Speak your truth. Your personal journey is a sacred gift to the betterment of the whole. If excessive pace is the problem, controlling your own is the cure.

Kevin Hancock is an award-winning author, speaker, and CEO. Established in 1848, Hancock Lumber Company, led by its 550 employees, is one of the oldest family businesses in America. The company is a six-time recipient of the "Best Places to Work in Maine" award. Additionally, Kevin has received the Ed Muskie Access to Justice Award and the Habitat for Humanity Spirit of Humanity Award.

Kevin's first book, *Not For Sale: Finding Center in the Land of Crazy Horse*, won three national book awards. His most recent book, *The Seventh Power: One CEO's Journey into the Business of Shared Leadership,* was released in 2020 and is available wherever books are sold.

Kevin is a frequent visitor to the Pine Ridge Indian Reservation in South Dakota and an advocate of strengthening the voices of all individuals—within a company or a community—through listening, empowering, and shared leadership.

www.kevindhancock.com
www.linkedin.com/in/kevin-hancock-6bb0501a1
www.facebook.com/kevindhancock/
www.instagram.com/kevindhancock/

History Rewritten by Choice

It has been said that beauty is in the eye of the beholder. Truth is, everything is perceived subjectively. Whether we consider something to be negative or positive, heartful or harmful, uplifting or devastating, is the result of it passing through our own perceptual filters. Valuing is done through our eyes—we are the beholder.

We yearn for the safety and comfort of relationships grounded in trust, business dealings bound in honor, and political leaders steeped in high integrity; yet our society is riddled with examples of betrayals on all levels. Distrust is ubiquitous. Our seeking exposes our vulnerability. Our sadness, when our misplaced trust is breached, triggers withdrawal—an actual biochemical production that interrupts our neural pathways and causes regions of our brains to disengage and shut down. Unbeknownst to us, these emotional pendula swings, from desire to withdrawal, etch neural pathways in our brains—the routes in which our habits are imbedded. Every thought and emotion have related neural pathways.

Apparently, I was born with a "generous spirit." I can't remember a time in which I didn't want to help and to give, whether it was nursing dolls, feeding stray animals, sharing my lunch, or giving away toys—or anything else that someone else might want or need. I was generous with my time, talent, and treasures. This, I was told, made me a "good person." But there was a naiveté interwoven in my generosity. I thought I could trust the people my generosity attracted to me. In hindsight, I think the word "sucker" was tattooed on my back where others could see it, but I could not. My magnetic attraction for manipulators set me up for betrayal. The hurt of betrayal got tangled in my generosity and morphed it into something weird yet normalized—"giving to get" was how life was conducted.

I had become a skillful manipulator—transformed from victim to perpetrator. This less-than-authentic behavior ironically had amplified my own vulnerability to it. Having been the victim of some master manipulators, never consciously would I have perpetrated manipulation on anyone else, yet there I was!

Over time, wanting to be wanted and liked, I had become a pleaser. To shield my loved ones from the consequences of their own choices and the hurtfulness of the world, I had shown up as Jeanne d'Arc to rescue them. Under the guise of helping people, I gambled on them, frequently risking my own financial wellbeing. The common themes were my low self-esteem, my fears of betrayal, rejection, and abandonment. I searched for something outside to offset my inadequacies and fill what I sensed was missing inside. Unconsciously, I feared that if I didn't please, rescue, finance, or in some other way create dependency on me, the people I wanted to have in my life wouldn't stick around.

What I wanted was for them to be strong, skilled, and empowered to create their own lives, fulfill their own dreams. Instead, I had entangled them in my insecurities. Rather than strength, I had fostered dependencies, and I tethered them to me financially so they wouldn't abandon me. Those behaviors failed to benefit any of us.

The brain creates neural networks in response to habitual thoughts, emotions, and behaviors. The magnetic effect of such networks attracted more betrayal rather than the healthy relationships and closeness I desired. It was as though I had cast a giant net to reel in betrayers—my teachers. And teachers they were. They taught me the precariousness of misplaced trust, of believing in circumstance, of handing off my power, and relying on forces outside myself.

Then came the awakening! It wasn't sudden thunder and lightning. It was more like erosion: The artificiality of my world came crumbling down revealing how I had misplaced faith in circumstances and passing people.

The biggest shift came when I reconnected with my spiritual path. Early on, I thought I was a misfit because I knew I was a spiritual being. Unintentionally, I allowed myself to take a detour and fell into an emptiness that nearly devoured me. "Miraculously," I awakened from my stupor. I remembered that I am an expression of Spirit and that my journey, regardless of my weird wanderings, was unfolding perfectly before me. I realigned with the power of Spirit in me, as me—a Power greater than I am—a Power that makes it possible to live authentically in healthy, trustworthy relationships. I discovered resilience—the capacity to recover quickly from difficulties, to embrace tenacity born of Love and the boundlessness that arises from interconnectedness and interdependencies of Oneness. I remembered that Divine Guidance makes Itself known everywhere, yet we must be alert to notice it and awake to know what to do with it.

Retraining my brain was much easier than I had presumed. All it took was to consciously use the repetitive process that had numbed me to what had driven my manipulative behaviors and the undesirable result of my neediness. I began to set new intentions and build new habits that support the life I choose to live. I construct new neural pathways every moment—granting myself the freedom to express creatively, authentically, and empathetically. I am now free to support others to live their lives in fulfillment of their dreams with no strings attached.

I shifted my perspective and rewrote my history. My perceptions changed. Instead of being the victim of betrayals, I became the eager student of many teachers. I opened to new ways of being. Keenly alert to how Spirit shows up everywhere, my life took on new meaning; and today, I am fulfilling what I perceive is my purpose: I facilitate others' awakening to their pure, radiant potentiality.

Therisia "Trish" Hall, M.Div., an international speaker and best-selling author, is the Spiritual Leader of Center for Spiritual Living Metro which serves the Greater Washington, D.C., Metro area.

Passionate for peace and committed to inclusivity, Trish founded Way2Peace, an organization dedicated to honoring the dignity of all life, expanding experiences of kindness and respect, and facilitating the release of prejudices and other limiting beliefs. She is a member of the Fairfax County Interfaith Clergy Council and Interfaith Council of Washington, D.C., as well as a founding member of Tysons Interfaith.

An educator, facilitator, and dedicated student of world philosophies, Trish has an ability to recognize commonalities by enhancing communication among diverse populations. She has been a presenter at the Parliament of World Religions and a panelist for World Association of Religions for Peace.

Blending authenticity, humor, and compassion, whether speaking to audiences or individual clients, she thrives on awakening the magnificence within all.

trishhall.unltd@gmail.com
www.trishhallunltd.com
www.cslmetro.org
www.way2peace.org

SAM YAU

Inner Garden

The Outer World

Since March 2020, we have been inundated with devastating news about our country and the world. The global pandemic is still ravaging, unabated, in many countries. Worldwide, almost fifteen million people have been infected; more than 600,000 have died. In the U.S., daily new cases have surpassed 70,000, a new record; more than 130,000 people have died. Thirty million jobs have been lost.

With the backdrop of the pandemic and more than 130 years after the emancipation of African Americans, racial prejudice still pervades in the hearts and minds of many people. The suffocation of George Floyd, with his neck pressed under the knee of a white policeman for eight minutes and forty-six seconds while uttering "I can't breathe" more than twenty times and being captured on camera in daylight, finally awoke the conscience of the general public and provoked a global movement against racial and social injustice.

Currently, in the United States, income and wealth inequality have reached a level that threatens the social fabric. Political polarization has paralyzed our government. Many important laws and regulations protecting our environments have been circumvented or dismantled by the current administration.

Every day each of us lives in a competitive world. Each of us lives through life's vicissitudes and challenges. Who among us has not suffered back-stabbing and setback in our career, and betrayal and heartbreak in our relationships?

Amid such darkness, we wonder: Are there bright spots left from which we can find light, solace, and peace?

The answer is yes.

In fact, there is a bright spot. It is created by you. It is always accessible to you because it is within you. Nobody can take it away from you.

The Inner World

We can only experience the outside world through our inner states of being. There is no objective reality. Different people respond to the same event in different ways. It is not what happens outside that matters to us. It is how we feel and interpret, and how we respond to an outside event that determines our well-being. This is the secret that has been taught and passed down to us for thousands of years from the world's major wisdom traditions.

There is an inner world within us, shaped by our life experiences, by what we believe about the world, about ourselves, and about our relationships with others. We experience the world through the lens of our internal realities.

Of all the beliefs that anchor us, the most powerful and positive knowing is this:

Love is the true nature of the universe.

The most foundational teaching from Christianity is "God is love." Endowed with the image of God, the essence of our soul is love. The Bible says, "The Kingdom of God is within you."

Buddhist meditation enables us to realize the nature of our minds as awareness itself, from which we come to taste the interconnectedness of all that exists. Compassion arises naturally from the experience of oneness.

The most profound percept about relationships is encapsulated in the Hindu greeting "Namaste," which means "I bow to the divine in you." Knowing this as a fact rather than merely a polite salute transforms any relationship we have with other people.

If we anchor our inner world in the direct knowing, or lived experience, or learnt belief of these spiritual truths, we have already secured the brightest spot in our life. We will have a constant source of love, peace, and strength for ourselves and anyone that comes upon our path. Our life becomes a beacon that shines upon the world. To change the outside world, we must first change our inner world with these spiritual truths.

Which World Matters Most

In the poem below, I use the inner garden as a metaphor to epitomize how our inner world shapes the experience of our external realities...

INNER GARDEN

By Sam Yau

There was a time you worried
people would not be kind,
life would deal you a bad hand.
There is a garden inside of you.
You are its sole caretaker.
You can plant flowers of love.
You can sow seeds of wisdom.
When your garden is safe,
your world is safe.
When it is beautiful,
your world is beautiful.
When it is peaceful,
you become a peacemaker.
Your happiness comes from within,
no one can take it away from you.
When you are full inside, you see
the half-full in the world and fill it.
You see the best in others,
so they show their best to you.
People will be drawn to you,
events will coalesce into what you envision.
Your outer journey takes you
to the four corners of the earth.
Your inner one traverses
across the universe.
There is no outside world.
Every time you look outward,
it is a projection.
Tend your garden well.
Live inside-out.
The world you experience
is within you.

Sam Yau is a retired business executive, splitting his time between managing his investments and writing poetry.

Sam has re-invented his life several times: from CEO of a billion-dollar corporation, to chairman of a corporate directors' forum, to chairman of a well-known center for personal growth, to a poet who writes about soul's journey, life's vicissitudes, trauma and healing, consciousness, science and spirituality, and mysticism.

Sam has an MBA in Finance with University of Chicago. A single parent living with his fourteen-year-old daughter in Laguna Beach, Sam enjoys music, hiking, and active travel around the world.

cyyau1@gmail.com
www.instagram.com/samyau_poetry/

NICOLE DICKS

The Great UNbalancing Act

I wish I could say that I am approaching middle-age, but instead I've been submerged in it for what feels to be quite some time. Actually, I'm drowning in it. Between the night sweats and hot flashes, trips to the chiropractor and CBD cream to soothe my aches and new pains, I'm a middle-aged woman balancing a job, household, two teenagers and husband. It's a fulfilling, sometimes messy, blessed life.

It's funny, really. Growing up, I never planned to get married or have kids. It wasn't because my upbringing had flaws. It was pretty idyllic. My parents taught me to rely on myself, get an education, travel the world, and focus on what made me happy. My mom always said, "People come and go, and you need to like and enjoy being around yourself **first**. You are your own best company." Then I met my soulmate and everything changed.

My husband is a wonderful man and a lot like my dad. He's a great co-parent to the kids; and in so many ways, my better half. He's my calm when my anxiety is spewing a storm within me and the one that never mentions how I've gained weight or grew a new hair out of my chin. To him, I'm always beautiful and (mostly) rational. He helps to keep me balanced, and that has been a good thing. But as I approach fifty, I'm beginning to think it's time to shake things up again. Let me explain.

From that first moment you hear that there's a baby growing inside of you, instinct kicks in and you become focused on more than your own needs and wants. You begin to plan. Each breath has a new meaning, and it's not air meant just for you: You are *living* and *breathing* and *being* for your unborn child. In my case, we weren't sure we could even get pregnant. So once I heard the news, my entire perspective changed about why I was placed on this planet. Luckily, after having my son, we were also able to have a beautiful baby girl two years later. A healthy, happy family of four.

As a mom, I wanted to be 110 percent available. I was sure, if I worked and parented, something would be half-assed. I also knew if my kids were in daycare, I'd be missing out on sharing experiences with them. I was selfish…I wanted to be included in those memories and photo albums and not have someone else raise them. I wanted to be at the zoo with them for the new stingray exhibit and be the one that rubbed sunscreen on their chubby little cheeks, telling them to keep their hats on. If one of their sandals fell off when they were running towards the giraffes, it should be me to pick it up and Velcro it back on their tiny, but chunky, flipper feet. And if they fell and skinned their knee, it should be me to kiss away the tears.

It wasn't always easy. With one salary supporting us, we ate a lot of spaghetti, entertained the kids by taking them to local parks in the summer and play areas at the mall when the temperatures dipped. At that time in our lives, we were adding water to the hand soap until the bubbles were almost gone. Food was not wasted and purchases were not made unless necessary. My working friends were always the best during this lean time and often bought me lunches so I could join them. The conversations were always fun during those lunches, but I often wondered if they felt sorry for me just a little. Secretly, I was jealous of their showered hair and new purses; but in my heart, I knew I was where I was supposed to be.

Fast forward to today with two teenagers underfoot, busy schedules, and constant activity swarming around me. Today, I'm not planning their day-to-day activities or calling moms for playdates. Instead, I'm waiting for a text to see if my son will even be home for dinner or if I should eat leftovers, alone, for the second night in a row. Recently, the house has become quieter and my role as the "heart of the household" has started to disappear into the backdrop.

It happens quickly, watching your children grow up. One moment you remember taking the training wheels off of their bikes and the next moment, you are watching them walk out of your house and jump into their friend's car, heading to a party of a friend whose name you can't recall and parents you don't know. One day, when you hug them, you realize you are looking **up** into their eyes because they are inches taller than you.

It all happens *so quickly.*

After years of focusing most of my energy, time, and restless nights on raising small humans, approaching the end of a job well done is daunting. Yes, I realize parenting doesn't ever go away, but the role changes. It changes because it has to. It means you've done all you can to provide a foundation for your children so they can venture off on their own. No one tells you that during this evolution, a part of you dies a little, leaving you feeling like you're lost on the side of the road with a dull, aching pain in your heart, uncertain of where to go and what to do next.

Now the Beam scale is unhinged, tipping back to the side that tells me it's time to reflect on where I am today and where I want to be as a middle-aged mom. I've become unbalanced, ready to take chances and go outside of my comfort zone, having no idea what lies ahead. I feel like I've created the world's most brilliant house of cards, looked at it in awe, and then a gust of wind knocked it down.

It's time to start over once again.

Nicole Dicks is an account executive at Cork Tree Creative, Inc., a full-service marketing and public relations agency in Edwardsville, Illinois. In her role, Nicole assists clients with their overall marketing needs by contributing website content, social media management, and more. Over the years, her work experience has included working for non-profits, start-ups, and nationally recognized corporations. At an early age, Nicole wrote plays, puppet shows, poetry and songs; she feels fortunate that she is able to continue her love of writing as a career. For many years, Nicole has kept a journal to capture the world around her. She has written stories about marriage, parenting, love, and loss.

Happily married for twenty-two years, today she's a mom to two teenagers who continue to test her patience and make her smile daily. She believes the answer to happiness is "do what you love and share good vibes with others."

www.corktreecreative.com
www.linkedin.com/in/nicole-dicks-15502b31
www.facebook.com/nwdicks

MARY LENIHAN

Let LOVE - LOVE Me

With this breath. PAUSE FOR LOVE in the midst of everyday life. There is a LOVE that loves me. No matter what. Always, Unwavering, Forever. Unhurried breath. RECEIVE. With this breath, I receive This LOVE. With this breath, I let LOVE ~ love me. I receive This Unwavering LOVE. I let This LOVE ~ love me. Unhurried breath. LOVE MYSELF. In this moment, right now, what does LOVE want to share with me? Unhurried breath. LOVE OTHERS. In this breath, as I truly let LOVE ~ love me, I will truly, love others. Unhurried breath. Love heals what I thought could not be healed; loves what I thought could not be loved.

You did it! You practiced Pause For LOVE. How simple is that? The greatest value of the Pause For LOVE practice is its ease of applicability in our everyday life stuff: communication, relationships, daily routines, and situations seeming large or small.

Yesterday at the store, a big woman walked by me having loaded herself down with a six-pack of beer and several bags of chips. Due to the pandemic the store required a mask, but she was not wearing one. I was a bit perturbed as she passed by me without social distancing. I will not mince words. My immediate judgments were, "She's already unhealthy (I presumed) and she's buying alcohol and salty, greasy snacks. It's people like her getting sick and making others sick!" Suddenly I paused as a flood of mercy washed away my judgments and LOVE whispered, "Have mercy, Mary. You do not know this woman's situation. Maybe she has lost her job. Maybe she's homeless. Maybe she can no longer take the repercussions that the pandemic has thrown her way. In this moment she's leaning on food and beverage. Haven't you done something similar in the past when you felt as low as you could go?"

LOVE was right on, hence it's *LOVE!* I saw her as an innocent child of LOVE and nothing can change that, not even salty snacks. Isn't it better I recognize the presence of LOVE within her than judge her unworthy? Which is more healing for us both? LOVE can change behaviors.

I approach the checkout and while unloading my cart, an inner pause awakens me as I realize I am ignoring the young woman working behind the counter. I look up at her and ask, "So how's your day going?"

"All right" she replies. "How about you?"

"I am having a pretty good day!" I respond. We chat a bit and laugh. She goes out of her way to make sure I can use my forty-percent coupon. I am grateful. Handing me my last bag, our eyes join. Love and grace are pouring from her wide-open eyes. As I receive love and grace, it's given—one in the same.

"You take care and be safe." She smiled behind her mask.

"Thank you. You too," I said.

One quick trip to the store, one Pause For LOVE and three souls encounter an unveiling.

How did the Pause For LOVE practice originate? One morning restless in my quiet time that's supposed to be all tranquil and holy, right? Why do we meditate? Is it to get beaten up by our ego? And how does that help with a better day, exactly? Yes, we are not to judge our subjective experience, instead watch the thoughts go by like clouds, but some days I am getting drenched! This was one of those days. As I efforted to make peace happen, I heard within, "Mary, stop trying so hard. Let LOVE ~ love you." And I did. I let LOVE ~ love me. Trying to make up my own "peace" ceased. I found rest. I found Mary.

Help and Healing Four Ways:

PAUSE. When you think "I don't have time to pause," notice the presence of an inner pause even while doing. Pausing saves time.

RECEIVE. Receiving LOVE can seem simple on one hand and a big hurdle to master on the other. What closes your heart to receiving? It can be an unconscious belief that you are unworthy of love. This is a lie. You are worthy, not because of your own efforts. You are worthy *because* LOVE ~ loves you.

LOVE MYSELF. If the words "love myself" seem self-absorbed or lead to unhelpful self-indulgence, it's okay to admit that you don't know how to love yourself. Who does? Let LOVE show you how.

LOVE OTHERS. People can be hard to love, usually because of our mistaken perceptions of who we think they are. But remember LOVE loves that person that you are not loving right now, as LOVE is loving you right now when you are being unloving! There's no way out of This LOVE thing. There's a fragment of our mind—not the brain—that has decided to "go solo," so to speak, without LOVE. Some call this the "ego." The result of imagining that it's even possible to leave LOVE, or be abandoned by LOVE, is a nagging sense of aloneness. You are not alone. LOVE is your companion. We are here to companion one another. To companion is to *be with.*

Imagine someone in your life right now who's a challenge for you to love. Pause. Let LOVE ~ love you. Receive This LOVE. Ask LOVE to show you how to love this person. Step back from good intentions or nice sounding ideas—no need to figure out the way to love. You will see the way to love as you let LOVE ~ love you. Once, I was guided to *see LOVE* loving someone who I was angry with and the anger fell away. I was then able to be a loving presence with this person. The problem was resolved.

Everyone's worth a Pause in the midst of everyday life. I can Pause For LOVE; wherever I am, whatever I am doing and whomever I am with. It's a practice. The choice is always mine. With this breath.

Mary Lenihan, M.S., is co-creator, co-founder of Pause For Inspiration, a 501c3 nonprofit public charity, operating since 2008. Pause is a practice in connecting with "Your Helpful Self—the LOVE and WISDOM in you," an inner resource for communication, relationships, and everyday life. Mary responded to the call to "inspire the dispirited," authoring three books including *Pause For Inspiration in the Midst of Everyday Life* and eight Pause Practices: Pause For Inspiration (adults), Kids Can Pause, Teens Can Pause, Parents Can Pause, Teachers Can Pause, Prisoners Can Pause, Veterans Can Pause and Pause For LOVE.

Mary teaches Pause to educators, students, healthcare professionals, business owners/employees, families, and ministers/congregations.

She earned an M.S. in occupational therapy with faculty honors from Washington University School of Medicine, B.A.s in psychology and dance and certified movement analyst from the Laban Institute of Movement Studies NYC. Mary created *Moving in The Pause* to get one's inspiration in motion!

www.PauseForInspiration.org
www.PauseForYourHelpfulSelf.org
www.PauseForLove.org
www.facebook.com/pauseforinspiration/
www.instagram.com/PauseForInspiration/

SANDY HEUSER

Be the Light

During my time as an IT leader, "Bright Spots" had been the name of the weekly email I sent to my team recognizing the good things that had happened during the week and my appreciation for their contributions. It was a "love" letter and gratitude journal all rolled up into one. I planned on it being a one-time thing, but my team responded so positively, I kept it up every week for many months.

I loved being a leader. It fed my soul to know I was able to help others discover their potential and pursue their dreams. Leading a team is like working with a professional sports team in the advice we give and the principles we practice:

When you're on the field, leave your egos at home. The team is more important than any one individual.

Leverage each other's strengths and compensate for any weaknesses or blind spots by working together as a team.

Be able to read the field and adapt accordingly. Change accelerates fast; you must pivot quickly.

Cross-train for more efficiency and higher performance but stick to your true passion and calling.

Every person on the team plays a critical role. Respect each person's contribution and be clear on each person's role.

Good sportsmanship is a must.

Learn the plays.

Call a timeout when you need to.

Challenge a call if you must but accept the outcome.

Practice, practice, practice.

Review the tapes. See where you could do better and focus on one thing you could do differently.

Remember the basics and go back to them if the team is losing focus or becoming fragmented.

Condition both the mind and body.

Pain is part of the process.

Everyone must be a believer. Having the right mindset is key to any success.

Look for opportunities to innovate—create new ways of doing things, new technologies.

Give credit to your teammates; take the blame yourself.

Celebrate the victories and learn from the defeats.

....And know when it's time to step down or step aside.

* * *

That day to step down came for me in the fall of 2014. I realized that my team needed a different leader and I needed a change. That following May I took a role that I knew nothing about and embarked on a new journey. It was the most transformative year of my life. They say that great rewards come from great risks, and that was true for me. But the rewards weren't what I expected and the risks were beyond scary.

The rewards came in the way of progress over perfection; in learning to be a support player rather than the star player; in learning to acknowledge that there were other more gifted individuals in the role; and that for me to succeed, I had to dig deep to find other ways to contribute and add value.

Being a high performer and high achiever, it was humbling. It was hard. And yes, even a little humiliating at times. But I learned to "honor the struggle," as Brendon Burchard would say in his book *High Performance Habits*[1], and I learned to fail forward. I discovered talents that I didn't know I had; I honed skills that I didn't know I needed. I had an opportunity to influence on a broader scale than ever before and elevate the training experiences for hundreds of top performers. In short, it became my dream job.

Until it wasn't. Life's funny that way.

---

1 Brendon Burchard. *High Performance Habits: How Extraordinary People Become That Way.* California: Hay House, 2017.

After a couple years and several organizational changes later, I again found myself in a new role at ground zero, square one, another new beginning: i.e., the support player, passing the ball down the field so that someone else could score and be MVP; the coach on the sidelines encouraging others to be their best; the cheerleader celebrating the victories.

But that's okay. I had learned my lessons. I had learned to be at peace. I had learned that my worth is not tied to my achievements, my title, or to others' perceptions of me. My worth is not defined by the number of "Exceeds" on my performance review or the size of my salary—though the more money the merrier! My value is inherent and non-negotiable. I learned "being" versus "doing." You can't put a price on that.

My experiences taught me the importance of working towards a goal without being tied to the outcome, of surrendering versus resisting, of seeing the beauty and gifts that only failure can bring, of placing more value on relationships than on results. I met some extraordinary people along the way, and I grew as a person. I'm grateful.

Don't get me wrong, I still want to achieve great things and excellence will always be a goal I strive for. However, at this stage of my life and my career, I realize that being a "Bright Spot" in someone else's life and shining a light on others' successes could be the highest calling one could have. Perhaps my greatest achievements have nothing to do with "me" at all.

So, if you ever find yourself questioning your value, your contribution to your organization, try counting the blessings you bestow on others. Measure the times you put in a good word for someone or helped someone else achieve—regardless whether you received any of the credit. Track the times you were a good friend or gave to someone who didn't have anything left to give, being the calm in someone else's storm, being a light and a spark of hope when all there is is darkness.

To me, that's what leadership is all about. Lighting a path for others and letting them shine.

Lord, help me to be a reflection of your light and love in the world, and help others to see the beauty and excellence in themselves so they can become the best version of themselves and live the life of their dreams.

Sandy Heuser grew up in a tight-knit family in a suburb of St. Louis where neighborhood kickball, lightning bugs, barbecues, family dinners, ballgames, and trips to the library filled her summers. Her upbringing fueled a love for art, music, books, sports, and puzzles.

A series of fortunate events led Sandy to a twenty-seven-year career in financial services where she followed her passions in leadership, design, user experience, and high performance. Ideas and innovation were hallmarks of her work.

Her interests include travel, photography, creative writing, deep conversations, and lifelong learning.

Sandy graduated with honors from the University of Missouri—St. Louis (bachelor's) and Webster University (master's). She holds her Series 7 and Series 66 licenses. She is actively involved in Arts and Education Council, United Way, and Professional Women's Alliance.

Sandy currently resides in St. Charles, Missouri, where she enjoys spending time with her family.

www.linkedin.com/in/sandy-heuser-004407
www.facebook.com/sandy.heuser.31

KAY UHLES

Magical Messengers of Metamorphosis

I love butterflies! These fancy flutterers can hijack my focused attention at any given moment to their corkscrew flight; I watch them with awe. Butterflies symbolize hope, rebirth, transformation—a need for change from present life to the next phase. And in 1999, they epitomized a metamorphosis for me in no uncertain terms.

Early in my life, I lived under the poverty line. A single parent and head of household, I played the roles of mother, father, chef, dish-washer, chief-financial-officer—you name it. I made many decisions; some good, some bad.

One of the biggest decisions I would ever make was whether to remain status quo or resume my education, full time, while living on a college campus. By the way, I was fifty years old by then and an empty-nester.

It wasn't an impulsive idea. I did the research, explored the options, weighed the evidence, prepared the best I could, took action, and relied on my gut. But I still had my doubts.

Throughout my decision-making processes, I often asked for guidance before going to sleep at night. I begged, "Show me. Please." One night, I had a dream, a nightmare, that I was hosting a going-away-to-college party in a house I had previously owned. My kids, parents, sisters, aunts, uncles, and cousins were all there and engaged in light-hearted conversation. Suddenly, the walls of the house began collapsing. One by one. Each wall fell, crashing down onto my loved ones. Within seconds the house had disappeared, falling into a deep crater, pulling each person down with it. In a flash all was gone: Possessions. Home. Family.

An omen?

With the nightmare still rattling in my head, I continued moving forward towards quitting my job and finishing school—but I questioned the wisdom to perhaps destroy my life and others' in the process.

On morning walks around the neighborhood lake, I would look for answers. It was October 1998 and the lake's surface mirrored the autumn leaves. Day after day, I'd return home to carry on with my busines with no more clarity than before.

By December, although my deadline to commit to the college was some months away, I felt the pressure and was still unsure what my final decision would be—should be.

Holidays came. The mall was crowded, as shoppers looked for the perfect gifts. I looked for bargains. I passed a calendar kiosk when I realized I needed a calendar to start the new year and to finish my days as a court reporter, as planned, in August. Having seen no 1999 calendars, I asked the clerk.

"I'm sorry," he said, "I have no more full-year calendars, but I have one academic calendar left. It goes through August. Half price."

A sign?

"I'll take it!"

I don't believe in coincidences, but rather in stepping stones, signs, affirmative nods, along a path. I was confused. If the dream of my collapsed house was an ill omen warning against moving forward and the calendar was a positive, which should I follow?

Unsure, I continued moving forward, taking action toward my goal.

January through July 1999 was consumed with depositions and transitioning my business from my own court reporting agency to that of a respected agency in the city. The owner and I had agreed that, under his umbrella, I would report and transcribe depositions; that I would turn over to him all other administrative duties—I would also turn over my clients. This was the point of no return.

By the end of July 1999, I had begun preparing my condo for the move: washing curtains, shampooing carpets, cleaning closets. Anything that would not fit into a nine-by-twelve room was discarded or stored.

Early August, two weeks before moving onto campus, I visited the nearest Laundromat with a comforter too large for my stackable washer. Behind the

Laundromat was a hardware store. After loading the comforter into the machine and depositing the requisite quarters, I walked around the block to purchase packing tape. On my return to the Laundromat, with my purchases in a bag swinging from my arm, deep in thought of my future, I rounded the corner when, **SMACK!** An object flew into my left thigh. *Was that a butterfly? Was that a butterfly?* Not seeing the fleeing flyer, I took a couple more steps. **SMACK!** It hit again—this time just under my right eye. *See me?* It snickered. I saw it. Plain as day. An agent of change. A butterfly.

No coincidences. Two out of three signs were positive. I hoped.

Mid-August, when I arrived at my college apartment, colorful construction paper cut-outs of autumn leaves and the names, "Jennifer," "Ashley," and "Kay," bid welcome.

Did I mention I was fifty years old at the time?

The second-story apartment was spacious with two bedrooms: one for my roommates, with bunked beds and two dressers; one for me, nine-by-twelve, just large enough—barely—for a single bed, dresser, and computer desk. The bed, a mattress covered in cotton ticking, was thin, gray, old; next to it, a window overlooking a single oak tree. A deck off the living room overlooked a lake and woods. Taking it all in, I envisioned the next two years—good or bad.

Once settled, I set out to explore the nature paths around the campus. Walking in the woods, the smell of fall and the school year approaching wafted with the musty smell of the thatch beneath my feet; the air, heavy with the manifestation of my goal. What had I done? Would my future hold financial promise and personal growth? Or financial ruin and regret?

It was getting late. I headed back, reflective.

The woods ended, and the path opened to a grassy meadow.

I stopped in my tracks in utter amazement.

In the meadow before me, hundreds upon hundreds of butterflies flaunted their yellow and orange wings in the golden afternoon light, flying corkscrews above the grass—magical messengers of metamorphosis.

I snickered and said, "I see you."

Kay Clark-Uhles is a writer, editor, consultant, teacher, and facilitator. She is a contributing author in the best-selling anthology, *Fearless and Fabulous: Finding Your Way through Change and Beyond*, released May 2020.

Kay is passionate about preserving memoirs and life stories. She believes that everyone has a story to tell! It's just a matter of sitting down and writing it—or finding someone to write it for you. Kay enjoys assisting new authors in finding and expressing their individual voices, her compassion for which stems from her educational and MI (motivational interviewing) experiences.

Kay is excited about the release of her first solo book, *Parts, Pieces, & Particulars: A Primer for Single Moms Raising Boys and Single Dads Raising Girls*, coming later in 2020.

Kay has a B.S. from Southern Illinois University and an M.Ed. from Colorado State University. She enjoys spending time with family, traveling, and watching butterflies.

KayClarkUhles.com
mindwise.soulworks@gmail.com
www.facebook.com/KayClarkUhles
www.linkedin.com/in/kay-clark-uhles

DAN PENNINGTON

The Lighthouse

Throughout history, light has taken on many forms. The first form of man-generated light was fire. This light was used for security, cooking, and illuminating the surrounding area. Over the years light became more refined with candles, gas lamps, and wood-burning stoves. It generated power for steam engines and kept homes warm. This same fire, in the form of lighthouses, gave ships a point of reference in storms and quiet waters to sail their ships safely home. Lighthouses were separated by miles; too many lighthouses could cause confusion and steer the sailor off course.

We all have to make a choice which lighthouse to follow in the toughest situations. I found myself at this crossroad during my first biomedical engineering job. I was twenty-three and my wife, Melanie, was six months pregnant with our first baby. I had been on the job about a year when I was accused of trying to steal an account from the hospital and was terminated. I appealed the charges to administration. And then the waiting game began. No job, no health insurance, and baby on the way.

To say I was stressed is an understatement. For three days I paced the floor of our apartment trying to find a solution, but no hope was found. At the end of myself, I looked to the Lighthouse of Jesus and surrendered my family to His guiding Light. The next day I got a call from administration that the investigation was over and I was found to be innocent of the charges against me. I was reinstated to my position and received back pay for the days I missed. Melanie gave birth to our beautiful daughter with all expenses covered by insurance. Once I surrendered to the Light of Jesus, He charted a course that met all of our needs.

In 2020 there are many who claim to be the lighthouse on which others need to place their focus. They promise safe waters, but the light they give, in my opinion, is often manufactured from their own arrogance and lack of wisdom. Because their words promise peace and security, I believe that many people listen to them and find out too late that the half-truths they proclaim are self-serving. To me, these guides—dimmed, diminished lighthouses—provide no clear direction and can lead followers to a deep pit that benefits them alone.

So, how do we determine what lighthouse to use as our guide to safe passage in these troubled times? First, let's investigate the lighthouse itself. Is their love for others unconditional? Have they sacrificed their time, money, and personal well-being? Is their integrity without question? These are just a few of the many questions that can be asked, but they all boil down to one question: Do they love others more than they love themselves?

The one person in history who I can answer "yes" to every one of these questions is Jesus Christ. I know that Jesus's love for me is not only unconditional but is at its best when I am at my worst.

The Bible says in Romans 5:8 that while we were still sinners, Christ died for us. This says to me that God saw all the sinful things we would do and still sacrificed His Son for us to be forgiven; that Jesus put His needs, wants, and survival on the table so that we could be saved from our sins, have a relationship with God, and have the security of knowing our eternity is with Him when our life on earth is done. This passage means that I can trust in the Light of Jesus. I do not have to question His motives for what He teaches me or the path He instructs me to take. I can be confident that His direction is for my good and not developed from selfish motives.

I believe that this is great news—that God not only provided Jesus, but also an instruction manual on how to follow in His steps. He provided this through His Word. To me, the Bible is God's bright flashlight in a dark world. When other lighthouses from this world scream to listen to them, I can look through God's Word to see if it shines His Light. If their messages line up with what the Bible says, I know it will be a help to me along my journey. The Bible guides my relationships, business dealings, and finances. It shows me how to live a life of contentment and not a grumbling life because I do not get everything I want. I see

God transform my heart to show compassion, love, forgiveness, peace, patience, and self-control. As I accept God's instruction in the Bible, I find a path that will build others up and not tear them down.

I believe that the whole of the Bible is summed up in one passage. Matthew 22:37-40 says to love God with everything we have and to love our neighbor as ourselves. Jesus said all the law and prophets hang on these two commandments. It is a path of finding what is good for somebody else instead of what is best for us. When I do this, I represent Jesus well and show those around me the love of Jesus.

In my earlier crisis, when I placed my trust in the Lighthouse of Jesus, God used the Light of His Spirit within me for guidance. My faith in Him became a landmark to help point others to the Lighthouse of Jesus! The Light of God's Spirit empowered me to see what His will is in my life. God's Spirit gives me wisdom in the tough choices and enables me to show the love of Jesus to others.

In a world filled with hopelessness, Jesus is a Light that corrects my ship's course when the waves of this world threaten to sink me. All I have to do is look to His Lighthouse as my guide.

Dan Pennington is a new author who has done most of his past writings in ministries local to the St. Louis, Missouri, area. He has been a biomedical engineer for the past twenty-six years. His home is in Wentzville, Missouri, where he is an elder at Wentzville Christian Church. He is husband to his beautiful wife, Melanie, and father to Brittany, Ben, Samantha, Nic, Lilly, and Seth.

Dan is excited to be a part of the Bright Spots team and hopes that his chapter contribution will be a blessing and encouragement to its readers.

Dan can be reached at danpennington@charter.net.

LISA A. WILLIAMS

Gifts of the Present Moment

Divorce. It happens to "other" people, not me. But it did. It was one of the two most difficult, life-changing times in my life, second only to losing my mother to cancer when I was eighteen years old.

In 2006, at forty years old, I had everything. Finally. So I thought. I got married in Vail, Colorado, on a mountain top—the wedding of a lifetime. Then, we bought our first house; something I had craved, having lived in only apartments and condos before. I enjoyed this beautiful place I called "home," with its luxury-hotel feel.

Then at forty-two, I gave birth to my one and only miracle: a perfect baby girl. Life was good. After her birth, I looked forward to birthdays, events, and holidays—planning tropical vacations, Thanksgiving with family, Christmas parties with Santa, lots of children, and all the goodies imaginable—all while working as a youth minister and planning future lessons and outings for my students. Life kept me busy planning and looking ahead. I did not focus on, nor was I aware of the present moment.

Life changed in 2016. My husband drank too much, was gone often, and had found comfort with someone else—i.e., my co-worker and best friend (I thought). It was devastating. I had been betrayed twice: once by my husband and once by my friend. The depth of pain I felt was enough to make anyone angry and miserable. It took a lot of therapy and wine to get me to a place of feeling somewhat "normal" again.

In 2017, I bought my own townhome. Trying to find my way, with my daughter, was arduous; but eventually, we settled into our new place. We also began to settle into a custody arrangement with her father.

Accepting the idea of having split custody with the ex-husband was more difficult than I ever imagined. Having to "*share*" my eight-year-old and not see her for several days was heartbreaking.

I remember the first time she spent "*shared time*" away from me. Early that morning, as I drove her to school, I could feel my heart sinking. I knew I would not be seeing her for five days. Perhaps we'd have phone calls, a short hello, but I wouldn't see her.

Oh! The angst of knowing she would be spending time with her dad and the woman who had betrayed me.

I kissed her head at the school yard. As she waved goodbye and headed into her classroom, I felt as though my heart was being ripped out of my chest. I barely made it back to my car from the schoolyard when I began sobbing. Would I ever feel like this would be "okay"?

Friends told me it would take time; they were right. It took quite a bit of time for me to get used to this new arrangement. But I did.

Trying to find "something good" out of **not** having my girl with me all the time was a struggle. I had to find ways to keep myself busy or do something that would bring me peace and a bit of joy.

When I was married, I focused on taking care of my daughter, husband, household chores, and work. My needs were put on the "back burner"; the idea of spending time on myself was a notion I was just beginning to open up to.

I started working out at the gym and noticed a yoga sign. I had done a few classes many years back but didn't stay with it. Well, I tried it and this time it stuck! That is when I embraced "being in the moment."

By being in the moment, I not only learned the yoga positions, but also was finally able to learn ways to nurture myself, to listen to my body. I was also one hundred percent available to listen to others. What a gift!

One day after realizing this gift, I had lunch with a friend. My phone vibrated with several texts. I was tempted to read them, but then I listened to my thoughts. *Put the damn phone down!* I realized that to be in the moment with my life-long friend and soul sister was invaluable and that I remembered those moments best because I had developed the awareness to be present—a practice I used that day and every day since to show love for all those around me.

As I look back at my life. I still see the divorce and ultimate shared custody of my daughter as the most difficult time in my life. And I know now that, because of this life-altering time, I was "called" to find strength and faith within my soul. I was able to tap into a Divine source and find peace. And through the practice of staying in the present moment, an ancient philosophy, I found that I am a stronger and more resilient woman than I ever thought I could be.

* * *

I invite you to bring peace into your life by living in the present moment through this simple meditation:

*Allow yourself to be in this moment, this gift to you. Close your eyes and notice your breath. Fill your belly with air, hold, release. Repeat two more times. This breathwork will bring you into the present moment. Be aware of your thoughts drifting by, departing your mind and body with your **out** breath.*

You are now connected to Divine source of love and peace, tranquil in this moment. Open your heart and mind to the unlimited possibilities of this moment. In your mind's eye, look around your natural environment and see the amazing qualities of nature that surround you.

Embody these qualities of peace, harmony, love, and balance in your body, mind and spirit. Create beautiful memories by being in the now. Be grateful for this present moment in time.

And so it is, be receptive to all the wonders of this Universe and the life experiences within it.

Reverend Lisa A. Williams, RScF, for the past thirty-five years, has inspired and empowered people of all ages, reminding each of the Truth, beauty, and gifts within themselves and others! Lisa is the founder of InnerDazzle, LLC, an enterprise designed to provide personal growth resources through spiritual coaching, workshops, seminars, webinars, guided meditations, Facebook Live Prayers, speaking engagements, and story-time events. Lisa also serves as officiant for weddings and baptisms.

Lisa is a native of Colorado. She lives with her daughter, Abigail, and their two kitties, Sugar and Sir Blue. Lisa is a fun-loving person, who enjoys traveling the world, trying new cuisine, and watching her daughter grow. She stays active by walking in nature, hiking, and practicing yoga.

Lisa and Abigail are co-authors of *Four Fabulous Fairy Tales and Mindful Mini Meditations*.

Lisa@InnerDazzle.com
www.Facebook.com/InnerDazzleLLC /
www.FB.me/spiritualresource
www.Instagram.com/innerdazzlellc
www.yourheartsdesirewedding.com
www.blackbirdsrising.org
YouTube Video: Four Fabulous Fairy Tales https://youtu.be/lpvY9qbK2cw

JOANNE WEILAND

An Outbreak of Love

My sisters and I have been part of a blended family for most of our lives. Our parents separated when we were teenagers. Dad kept our thriving family business; Mom received half of the portfolio and has been married to a wonderful man for the past thirty-four years. Our dad has not been as fortunate with relationships. Some women he dated had children who came first and enjoyed spending his seeming abundance of ever-flowing cash, cars, and carefree lifestyle. One woman hung around for over a decade before she made her get away with all of Dad's earthly belongings and money.

Christmas was an especially emotional holiday. We would all gather at Dad's place, including—well—*her* son. Most of us would each receive one gift. For example, one year my gift was a plastic mirror. However, the son could hardly drive back home; his entire car was filled with Christmas gifts.

One day Dad came home to an empty barn, bank account, garage, and house. I admire *her* for being such a planner. I often wondered how many people it took to help *her* take, pack, and haul everything away in nine hours. She didn't have friends, but you can hire movers.

Several years later, I decided to find our new mom myself. I invited my good friend and my dad for Thanksgiving dinner. They got along splendidly! Next, I invited my friend to go on a cruise with me. She accepted my invitation; we booked the weekend getaway cruise for January 2000. Unfortunately, the day before departure, I suddenly came down with some unknown, unheard of sickness (wink wink). What happened next? I quickly called my dad and asked if he would go on the cruise in my place. He said, "Sure." So, my friend and Dad spent the extended weekend on the cruise together and came home laughing, then started dating. Nine months later, they married. Success! I had chosen our new mother!

Fast forward eighteen years—our dad and step-mom, my friend, separated and lived apart for two years. Then the pandemic hit in early 2020. We had heard about this dreadful virus but had not experienced it until…

July 23, 2020, we got the call that our dad was in the hospital. The next morning it was confirmed—the pandemic had struck.

Eventually, his fever broke. We planned for discharge. Surprisingly, the next morning the doctor recommended a ventilator.

It is common for patients of this nasty virus to appear to be getting better and then quickly taking a turn for the worst. Our dad had sixty to seventy percent "ground-glass" opacities per lung—a signature of the global outbreak. Within a matter of hours his respiratory system had declined to the point of needing the ventilator! My sisters and I gave consent, and before the procedure, arranged for a video chat. But at lunch time, the three of us were told they were intubating him "now." So, no video chat.

There were three days where the doctors gave us no hope and would not even discuss discharge. Some people suggested my sisters and I start making "arrangements," but we kept believing and praying and singing a hallelujah. We knew our dad would be brought back to us.

Dad was on the ventilator for four days—until he decided he did not like it. So, on August 1st, when the ICU nurse was not looking, he pulled the ventilator tube out himself (with the bulb still inflated). Hearing this, the doctors wanted to reintubate him. Fortunately, they found that his heated high-flow oxygen was sufficient.

Throughout this ordeal, Dad became very confused, and the doctor told us they could not guarantee that his mental function would return. Doc said they are finding that the mental rehabilitation for all of their ICU patients (not just pandemic victims) was as bad or worse than the physical rehabilitation as a result of going through these experiences without loved ones by their side. Once again, God showed up.

Sadly, our bonus mom (step mom) developed the virus also and was admitted to the same hospital on August 4th, soon after our dad had extubated himself. She had a milder case, so they allowed her to visit his room, which helped immensely (So thankful!). Then we were called and told that the insurance company was changing its policy with this global outbreak, and they would need to discharge her because her case was not severe enough to require hospitalization; she would be sent home with observation only.

Then she developed the illness in her lungs and required oxygen. She was able to stay with our dad! On August 10th, they were both transferred to a rehab center in Greenville, South Carolina, to gain their strength and, God willing, be going home soon. One night my sisters and I talked to both of them on the phone, and Dad's mental capacities were much improved.

My sister Susie has taken care of the elderly as her professional occupation for thirty-five-plus years. I totally admire her because I volunteered to take care of our dad and bonus mom in South Carolina after their release from the rehab center. I had hitched a ride from Tampa, Florida, with my thoughtful nephew in his Peterbilt twenty-two wheeler. He had a job eighteen miles away from our dad's home! It was fun seeing the country from a new vantage point for nine hours.

As of this writing, I am the caregiver and will be for a few more weeks. The "Bright Spot" is that our parents are regaining their strength and have been reunited.

There were many other miracles of healing in that month, including our dad and bonus mom being reunited and deciding to live together again as husband and wife! My sister Debi says: The message is, whatever your battle is, raise a hallelujah and give Him praise! God is good all the time!

Joanne Weiland created the Collaboration Cloud Community LinktoEX-PERT to connect executives, entrepreneurs, and event professionals in order to join forces and implement their ideas with ease.

Freelancers secure more projects and speaking engagements, and create additional streams of income on LinktoEXPERT. These professionals create their messages and LinktoEXPERT distributes them, via its Unique Database Exchange Program, to decision-makers worldwide.

Executives and entrepreneurs utilize LinktoEXPERT to find experts, review their credentials, and hire experts in minutes to complete their projects. Joanne persistently master minds, mind maps, and builds relationships globally. She was a "growth hacker" before she knew that measuring marketing results was growth hacking.

Joanne is regularly interviewed on podcasts and radio shows worldwide.

She encourages everyone to "Do what you love and love what you do."

Her motto: *Be seen. Be heard. Be known worldwide with ease!*

www.LinktoEXPERT.com
Safety Harbor, FL 34695

ROBERT U. MONTGOMERY

Showered with Blessings

During August, my least favorite month, the Perseid meteor shower serves as my bright spot. In the late-night hours, I forget about the heat, humidity, and bugs as I gaze at the shooting stars. With crickets and tree frogs harmonizing in the dark woods around me, I marvel at the celestial beauty, give thanks for another year, and count my blessings.

Blessings aren't elusive. Because they make us happy, they're easy to recognize. Usually.

But this year has been like no other for me. And not just because of the global pandemic and its impact. Consequently, it's taken me a while to understand how blessed I have been during this summer of the shutdown.

At the beginning of the pandemic, because of their vulnerable clientele, senior centers were among the first to close, including the one where I had been volunteering for more than nine years. The homebound, however, still needed assistance, and so the Meals on Wheels program continued. In fact, demand grew, even as we lost volunteers with pre-existing conditions who feared for their own well-being.

As someone who had been blessed with good health, I helped pick up the load, distributing meals twice or even three times a week for more than a month.

And then it happened. One week I delivered meals; the next, I was receiving them as I suddenly began to experience the most painful summer of my life. In fact, until I endured it, I had no idea that such gut-wrenching misery could even exist. Of course, I never had a back injury either. I since have learned that most all of my friends have experienced similar ailments and that back pain is common. But I had no idea.

117

As I wound my way through the medical maze of pills, therapy, and referrals, searching for relief, I barely could walk or stand. I couldn't sleep, shower, shop, walk my dog, or drive myself to medical appointments. And, except for Pippa, my canine companion, I lived alone.

I've always been an independent sort, rarely, if ever, asking others for help. I took pride in assisting others, while being able to take care of myself. But that paradigm no longer was valid. I needed help.

And my friends and relatives were there for me. Don't get ahead of me, though. The blessing bestowed upon me during this summer of pain is about a lot more than their kindness and generosity, although those are significant.

As they picked up prescriptions, helped with laundry, walked Pippa, shopped, drove me to appointments, and even cooked for me, they did more than just help meet my physical needs. That's why, despite the near constant physical pain of more than three months, my spirits never have sagged.

Before all of this happened, if you had asked me how I would feel about so many people doing so much for me, I would have said, "Not good. I don't want to be dependent on anyone."

Sure, I understood how volunteering benefits those who give as well as those who receive. I know with certainty that delivering Meals on Wheels made me a better person. I started doing it because I thought it was a "good" thing to do for others. But over time, the people that I delivered to and the people I delivered with became my friends. And I recognized in me a kinder, more forgiving, more patient, more generous, and more thoughtful person.

When I saw that he didn't have enough money to buy the basics of milk, bread, and meat, I paid for the groceries of a man in front of me at checkout. In the parking lot of a thrift store, I saw an older woman pushing a table toward the street. Her intent was clear and frightening. With no other alternative, she was going to try to manhandle the table across the road, despite nonstop traffic. I took a quick right into the parking lot, and, with her permission, loaded the table into my car and opened the passenger door for her. I drove her home, where I unloaded the table and took it inside.

Over the years while delivering meals, I fixed vacuum cleaners—or attempted to anyway—and opened pill bottles. I moved furniture, adjusted television settings, and gave rides to those who needed to get to appointments or buy necessities. Also, I recognized that some people needed the human contact as much as they needed the food, and I might have been the only one they talked to that day.

But I didn't realize what it felt like to be one of those people. And you know what? It feels pretty good, especially when those assisting you are friends and relatives. When they bring you care packages, when they carve a watermelon, when they not only wash and dry your clothes but fluff them, when they show up on Taco Tuesday with—what else?—tacos, you know that you are loved. And whatever pain that you are feeling physically is diminished by the mental, emotional, and spiritual lift provided by that love.

And so, as I sit here, watching heavenly majesty light up the August sky, awaiting microsurgery in a few weeks, I understand and embrace the elusive blessing that has been bestowed. During my summer of pain, friends and relatives have shown me that something is more important and, in the process, lessened my suffering considerably.

Yes, doing for others feels good. But when you're injured, lonely, or anxious, never be afraid to ask for help. Friends and relatives are there to care for you and lift you up, just as you are there for them. They do so not just with deeds, but with love, as they give you the strength and incentive to endure.

Doing for others is not enough, especially during troubled times. You must also ask them to do for you. Together, we make the world a better place.

A former teacher and writer about nature and the outdoors, Robert U. Montgomery is author of a dozen books, including two novels. During the past two years, he has written *Nourishing the Soul: The Real Value of Meals on Wheels* as a fund-raiser for local senior centers, along with *Who Let the Dinosaurs Out?* and two other illustrated children's mysteries, which teach kids about nature and encourage them to go outside and explore.

Robert's latest book, *Big Sam and the Big Out*, will be out later this year. He wrote it as a tribute to his friend, Sam Griffin, a legendary bass fishing guide and luremaker on Florida's Lake Okeechobee.

Montgomery's other offerings include *Pippa's Journey: Tail-Wagging Tales of Rescue Dogs*; *Fish, Frogs, and Fireflies: Growing Up with Nature*; and *Under the Bed: Tales From an Innocent Childhood*.

You can find his work at rumpublishing.com and Amazon.

roticomontgomery@gmail.com
www.rumpublishing.com
www.linkedin.com/in/activist-angler/
www.twitter.com/Rumpublishing
www.facebook.com/roticomontgomery/
www.facebook.com/authormontgomery
www.facebook.com/fishfrogsfireflies
www.amazon.com/-/e/B005J1K9T2

From Overnight Success to Rock-Bottom

"A man isn't finished when he's defeated.
He's finished when he quits."

— Richard Nixon

I've always had an uncanny knack for making my dreams and goals a reality. Some say it's manifestation, determination, and yet others say it's dumb luck. But regardless of how it's defined, it's real; and I've walked a long road towards learning how to use this skill responsibly.

You see, most people—everyone, I daresay—HAS this skill. Yet, so few of us learn to use it properly, and the process of doing so will require your ego and pride to take a backseat.

My most painful and compelling lesson in this came at the cost of millions, literally. I was twenty-one, fresh-faced, and full of all the wisdom a young man of that age THINKS he knows, and just enough life experience to validate it to myself. I'd drop out of college and started my own business, forming mutually beneficial relationships between high-end investors and start-ups looking for financial backing. With my uncanny luck, it wasn't long before I'd formed an incredibly lucrative partnership between two clients worth upwards of $300 MILLION at its completion!

But lacking the maturity to wait for my contract to prove itself, I became the classic party boy living and buying like that paycheck was already mine. I went shopping for three-piece designer suits, joined exclusive clubs, and bragged to friends and family. I made a general jerk of myself. My lack of patience and true wisdom came back to haunt me when the business partnership fell through, leaving me with nothing but red numbers in my finance accounts.

I. Was. Humiliated. At first, it was easy to fake my way through being okay while drinking away the anger and fear. Eventually, though, my fragile grasp on control caught up with me, and I slipped over the edge into rock-bottom as I lost the last bit of business I'd been surviving on.

But one of the silver-linings of rock-bottom, I realized, is you have nothing to lose in trying something new. I had a chance to hit the reset button with greater foresight and maturity than I'd shown before—IF I was willing to take full responsibility for who I'd been and who I wanted to become.

Finally, I was asking myself the important questions. What kind of man would I be *proud* to become—not for my money, car, and good fashion sense, but for the *real substance* I was made from?

The answer came quickly. I was going to travel the world for a year, taking only what would fit into a backpack, while using my website design and building skills to finance my journey of re-creation. I'd also heard about a ten-day Silent Vipassana Meditation Retreat and knew it'd be the perfect way to break the damaging habit of self-avoidance and escapism through alcohol before my travel began.

During the retreat, we spent ten days without technology, substances, stimulants, touching, or any communication aside from the staff's guidance to fully face and feel everything you tend to avoid. The retreat accomplished its purpose as I faced all the layers in my now twenty-four years of life. It wasn't pretty, but that inward isolation took me back to the raw truth of who I was beneath the years of acting and being who I thought the world wanted me to be.

I left there taking what I knew to be true back into the world:

> *"Life isn't about finding yourself.*
> *Life is about creating yourself."*
> — George Bernard Shaw

I journeyed all across the United States, into England, Europe, Spain, Brazil, and beyond as each destination peeled away more layers, revealing who I was becoming. Each night in a new location—be it a cheap hostel in a room full of strangers or the couch of a willing friend— tenderized my ego, giving me a clean canvas on which to see myself.

The freedom, stability, and humility gained by living simply and honestly painted me in textures and colors MEANT to reflect the truth of my soul. The various cultures, locations, traditions, and experiences worldwide added depth and dimension to my roughness and sharp edges. The friendships, laughter, conversations, and intimacy shared with kindred spirits added a richness to my being worth far more than any money can buy. My homelessness and minimalism gave me an understanding of real privilege and perspective in realizing I am no better or worse than anyone else.

We're all doing our best with what we have and who we believe ourselves to be. My lack of roots and rest showed what "Home" truly means; and in the emerald hills of Oaxaca, Mexico, those roots ached to settle in place and grow.

With my lessons reflected on and learned from, I channeled my uncanny luck into recreating not only myself, but my life and career as well. That year changed my life for the better in every way, and if there's one takeaway I aim to share, it's this:

Be willing to get uncomfortable. Challenge your views, thoughts, and known truths every day.

Don't fear and run from the chaos in your mind, body, and soul. Sit with it, relate to it, explore it, and use it to recreate yourself. You may be surprised at what *truly* brings meaning and joy in your life hidden in its dark depths.

Travel, learn from other ways, other cultures, all that has come and gone before you. Find the roots your soul has been aching to sink into.

But above all, remember that life isn't about *finding* yourself. It's about *creating* yourself to be truly YOU.

Adam Cortez is a strategist and systems creator for both business owners and leaders ready to take control of their lives. He has dedicated his business to supporting and creating powerful changes in his clients' lives so they have the time and energy they need to be the leaders they are capable of.

With over 15 years in marketing and project management, Adam has built ARC Websites to help clients create meaningful connections online and grow businesses from 0 clients to 100's of clients.

His strategies have been used to re-engage lost customers, gain Fortune 500 contracts, develop strategic partnerships, and close deals worth $300 million for companies.

www.facebook.com/arccreativeco
www.twitter.com/arccreativeco
www.arccreativeco.com/

YONASON GOLDSON

How Do You Respond to Chaos? Count Your Blessings!

Social distance. Shelter in place. Stay home and save lives. Wear your mask. These protocols have constituted the communal response as the 2020 pandemic has reshaped our lives under the new rules of contagion.

But how should we respond *introspectively*?

We don't have to figure it out on our own. History provides a template—one as relevant today as it was at the dawn of civil society.

Nearly 3,000 years ago, toward the end of King David's reign over the Kingdom of Israel, a mysterious plague swept through the population, striking down victims in vast numbers. The sages recorded that David responded by issuing a decree, a mandate that every person in the land recite one hundred blessings a day. Miraculously, the plague ended as suddenly as it had begun.

What Is a Blessing?

The Hebrew word for "blessing"—*bracha*—is related to the word *bereicha*, meaning a spring-fed pool. At first glance, these words appear unconnected. But there is literally more here than meets the eye.

Consider how life-giving water surges into the world from unseen reservoirs and wellsprings. In the same way, both the material resources that sustain us and the innate abilities that enable us to live rich and rewarding lives flow into the world from a hidden psychological and metaphysical source. To pronounce a blessing is an acknowledgement that we are beneficiaries of these gifts, as well as a declaration of our intent to show appreciation by using them to the fullest.

In the days of King David, the people suffered from a corrosive sense of entitlement. They took for granted the opportunity they enjoyed for using material prosperity to promote spiritual growth. The plague that descended upon them was a wake-up call, a reminder of how fortunate they truly were and of the responsibilities that come with affluence and freedom.

History Repeats Itself

In the days of this global health crisis, doesn't this sound awfully familiar? Hadn't our pre-pandemic abundance and well-being made it easy for us to forget the universal values that govern a healthy society and sustain vibrant and prosperous communities? Isn't the disruption wrought by the pandemic on our comfortable lives a stinging admonition to remember and recount our blessings?

The responses might seem obvious. The problem with the *obvious*, however, is that it blends into the background of our lives until we no longer notice it and forget it was ever there. Recounting our blessings prompts us to regain our bearings and restore grace to our lives in ways that should be second nature. Here are a few examples:

Add Depth to Discussions

Once social distancing forces us apart, we realize that staying connected takes real effort. In our age of hyper-connection, we had become comfortable with shallow exchanges and trivial conversation. By making us aware of our emotional isolation, quarantine drives us to seek deeper and more meaningful interactions.

Reach Out to Neglected Friends and Family

Accelerated by technology, the pace of life has convinced us that we need to continuously create new connections, often at the expense of old ones. Suddenly, we feel compelled to resurrect lapsed relationships. That's a good thing. But the real challenge will be remembering to continue nurturing the connections most important to us once the crisis has passed.

Look for Opportunities To Do Acts of Random and Calculated Kindness

Wash some dishes. Make the beds. Pick up a few toys. Do a load of laundry. Even when restrictions relax, don't take home for granted. Look for opportunities to lighten someone else's burden. Leave Post-It notes with upbeat messages stuck to the pantry door, the medicine cabinet, and the kitchen faucet for loved ones to find, or on a colleague's computer screen. Send short emails to acquaintances to let them know you're thinking about them. It takes little effort to brighten someone else's day.

Look After Your Physical and Spiritual Health through Exercise, Meditation, and Journaling.

More and more, science is revealing the practical benefits that physical activity and thoughtful reflection have on every aspect of our personal wellbeing. Our bodies and minds are gifts. Don't they warrant our attention and investment?

Seek To Spread Inspiration Rather Than Stewing Over Misfortune

As a rule, people don't complain because they're unhappy; people are unhappy because they complain. You don't like listening to other people kvetch. How does it affect your frame of mind listening to yourself bemoan your fate from morning to night? Conversely, the Jewish sage Shammai the Elder famously taught, "Greet every person with a pleasant expression." That includes that way you greet yourself in the mirror each morning.

But don't stop there. When you smile at a stranger, the stranger smiles back. Instantly, your whole world gets brighter. Before you know it, you can't keep count of the smiles and pleasant words that are coming back your way.

Mindset Is Everything

Often, the difference between a blessing and curse depends not on what happens to you, but on how you respond. It doesn't take much to shift your perspective. And once you do, you can't help but notice the sun shining through the clouds.

How do you shift perspective? Make a habit of asking yourself these questions every morning and every evening:

- What is one good thing that happened to me in the last twenty-four hours?
- Who is one person in my life I'm grateful for?
- What is one way my life today is better than it used to be?
- How can I express appreciation to someone who deserves it?
- What small action can I take to spread light to another person, right now?

The Hebrew term for "gratitude" is *hakores hatov*—literally, *recognizing the good*. When you notice the good in your life, your natural reaction is gratitude. All you need to do is pay attention; before you know it, blessings will begin to fall from your lips all by themselves.

Yonason Goldson is director of Ethical Imperatives, LLC, teaching leaders and professionals how good ethics is good business and the benefits of intellectual diversity. He's a keynote speaker, TEDx presenter, and community rabbi, as well as a repentant hitchhiker, recovered circumnavigator, former newspaper columnist, and retired high school teacher in St. Louis, Missouri. He's the author of hundreds of articles applying ancient rabbinic wisdom to the challenges of the modern world and five books including *Proverbial Beauty: Secrets for Success* and *Happiness from the Wisdom of the Ages.*

www.yonasongoldson.com/
www.linkedin.com/in/yonason-goldson/
www.facebook.com/yonasongoldson/
www.twitter.com/yonasongoldson
www.instagram.com/yonasongoldson/

DIXIE BENNETT

The Feminine Pathways to Prosperity

Women-driven businesses are the way of the future! At least that's my belief. As a collective, women are hungry for a new way of leading, innovating business, and measuring success. This is a different energy than the women of our ancestors and the timelines of feminism and suffragist movements. We are illuminating the way for more women to have their voices heard and are cultivating cultures of collaboration where the cycles of womanhood are celebrated and supported, making room for both business and family success.

As more soulful women step up and run their own businesses, innovation is taking shape with a combination of two powerful ingredients—servant leadership and sacred commerce.

The first ingredient of women-driven business is servant leadership. I'm not sure when this came into my awareness, but I have always thought it important. The more I explored it, the more it resonated with me. I recognize now that servant leadership was a part of my earlier corporate careers—and it served me well.

I had been a leader from behind the scenes. I had supported managers, VPs, executives, CEOs, and other successful leaders, globally, who were in the limelight. During that time, I was surrounded by millionaires, billionaires, and I received tastes of true wealth; but on the inside, (although fleeting) I felt there had to be more. I sought out and looked for teachers and mentors to guide me.

When I think of women servant leaders of today, I see Sarah Blakley, who runs Spanks, a billion-dollar business, and who created a culture around hiring women who nourish their careers and their families. When women make money, they find ways to stretch it and put it to use developing communities, hiring staff, and offering services.

In my twenties, I had three near-death experiences that stopped me dead in my tracks. In working on myself thereafter, I discovered that money, monetary gain, and titles weren't enough success for me. Then I received a whisper from Spirit that told me to open up a healing center. I knew that teaching and supporting others satisfied me, but it was through the launch of my business that I discovered the freedom to serve from a new energy. I was introduced to many other healers and empowered women who were building amazing businesses and creating global impact through collective collaborations. This world was different compared to the one I knew in the male-driven corporate world; it continues to intrigue me today.

I work with many women leaders from around the world and am still in the role of servant leadership. I still lead and support from behind. I remember years ago listening to Oprah. She shared that one of her practices was praying and asking how she could be of service every day. Many women in my circles have shared with me that when they lose their way or feel like life is too dark or hard, they take their children and volunteer at a shelter. I've used this too. When life feels hard, energy shifts; doors open when we put our services to work in other ways.

When we serve from our hearts, opportunities, new clients, and money always flow. Whenever I find myself swept up in comparing others' fortunes or looking for more money, I remind myself to go back to basics, to be of service, and to remind myself WHY I got into the business of serving others. I ask myself: Where and how can I be of service right now?

Good leaders must become good servants. This is evidence—if you are open to seeing it.

The second ingredient of feminine leadership is sacred commerce, that is, our relationship with money. I, personally, have had an interesting relationship with money. I've always made it; and it's always come easily to me, both in the corporate world and in entrepreneurship. I believe that women are masterful fertilizers that stimulate growth; we are natural community builders, networkers, seekers of solutions, and problem-solvers. We are resourceful and never stop moving forward.

When we shift our relationship to receiving money, stop undercharging or giving away services, and learn to ask for the sale, our lives flourish in many ways.

We live in a society that requires money, yet many women struggle with money. I hear women describe money as a "thing," an obstacle. If they just won the lottery, everything would be better. They dream about what they would do with a windfall that might land in their laps; they make lists of the life they would have and the things they would buy. Some wish that money didn't exist. They struggle paying their bills. When these limiting ideas shift to an abundance mindset, the money game will change.

* * *

I share with you my favorite prosperity tips. Follow these tips and watch for the rewards! You may be surprised at what you see.

Prosperity Mindset #1—When you make a purchase that supports another small business, imagine that money paying for their space, products, services, and paycheques; imagine the prosperity that pays for their lifestyle, kids, education, rent, groceries; and imagine that money rippling out into the world with blessings and goodness. Money is a never-ending thread; it moves, changes hands, and creates waves of opportunities.

Prosperity Mindset #2—When you're making payments—credit cards or bills—take the time to review the list of purchases shown, sit in gratitude for what those purchases had brought. For example, the Internet bill gave you full access to cell phones and computers; it provided connection to your family, friends, business opportunities, et cetera. Then, for every item on your statement, list ten more things to be in appreciation or gratitude for. Think of each payment as an investment in your life or business. This will enhance your relationship with money.

When money is appreciated, perspective changes and more opportunities will come.

Where and how can you be of service right now? And what is your relationship with money?

Dixie Bennett, soulful woman, wealth coach and healer, international speaker and best-selling author, and host of the "Inspired Women Gathering Show," is on a mission to empower one million women leaders who know they are meant for more and that life is not supposed to be hard.

Eleven years ago, after Dixie had experienced three near-death experiences and deep healing, Spirit directed her to leave her oil and gas career in international sales and marketing. She was guided into the healing and coaching arts, opening a transformational healing center called "Stillpoint Bodyworks," where she helps soulful women from all over the world clarify their vision, embody their true purpose, step into their visibility, and craft their sustainable, profitable soul-satisfying business. Dixie believes when women leaders align to their inner wisdom, bringing consciousness into their spirituality and businesses, they soar in their souls' purpose. This is the pathway to feminine prosperity.

www.facebook.com/groups/InspiredWomenGathering/
www.youtube.com/channel/UCEphNqiuKbpHSTVsXZMPsIA
www.facebook.com/iamdixiebennett
www.instagram.com/iamdixiebennett/
www.linkedin.com/in/dixiebennett/
www.stillpointbodyworks.ca/
www.dixiebennett.com

The Pit

"You will never underestimate the amount of pain someone else is in."
"Most people just want someone to listen…without judgment."

My mentor gifted me these words of wisdom during my life-coach certification. The longer I coach, the more important these words become.

Suffering can be overwhelming. Often inducing feelings of insignificance, isolation, anxiety, disgust, and despair. It can seem as though we are trapped, alone, and at the bottom of THE PIT with no way out. Most people don't like feeling pain or watching others experience it, so there can be an immediate reaction to stop, avoid, or lessen the pain.

When we see others suffering, stuck in THE PIT, there are several ways we can react. Some are easy, most are safe, but only one offers a bright spot of connection, affirmation, and safety—all of which are needed for healing.

Let's take a look at seven reactions so you can be more aware of them in yourself and in others as you connect with those who feel trapped in THE PIT.

Ignore

We see suffering, but choose to disengage. We insist it doesn't exist and eliminate our exposure by walking away.

Sounds like silence.

Apathy

We see suffering but choose safety over action. We go about our day, detached, indifferent, and unaffected.

Sounds like: "Hope you figure it out."
"It is what it is."
"I can't solve it, so why do anything?"
Distant silence.

Dismiss

We see suffering, but know better. People in pain don't understand their situation. From our superior perspective, we tell them how they should feel, minimize their suffering, and urge them to move on.

Sounds like: "It'll all be over soon."
"It's not so bad."
"Suck it up."
"Look at all the good..."
"Could be worse..."

Redirect

We see suffering but quickly shift attention to something we are comfortable engaging in. We don't publicly acknowledge or affirm anything and view those who expose their suffering as selfish for drawing focus from issues we care about.

Sounds like: "But what about..."
"Everyone is suffering."
"How can you be so selfish?"

Hijack

We see suffering but make it about us. We control our level of discomfort and exposure to pain by talking about our experiences. We dominate the conversation with our perspective and knowledge. We talk without listening. We believe our perspective and experiences are universal and position ourselves to be guide and savior.

Sounds like: "I'm hurting too. Let me tell you how I'm doing."
"I went through the same thing and know exactly what you're going through."
"This reminds me of when I..."

Fix

We see suffering and take immediate action to stop it. We don't believe people can handle their pain in a manner and speed that we are comfortable with, so we take control and tell them what to do. This requires effort and can lead to resentment for those suffering.

Sounds like: "The problem is really..."
"If it really bothers you, all you have to do is..."
"The solution is RIGHT THERE! Why can't you see it?"
"When you're ready to fix this, we can talk."

We often choose the six reactions above because:

They protect us from the messiness of suffering, require low risk, and ask for minimal effort. We control our exposure to pain, manage allocation of our resources (time, talents, treasures, connections, and opportunities), and refocus attention on ourselves while staying safely out of THE PIT.

Consequences of those reactions:

People who are vulnerable enough to expose their suffering are rejected and further isolated and may begin to question if they matter. They may adopt feelings of insignificance, a sense of low personal worth, and a victim mindset as they hide their pain. They may experience guilt, shame, or self-condemnation for speaking up and retreat deeper into THE PIT. Bold action may or may not be taken as a cry for attention, affirmation, and help.

The first six reactions have similar motivations and consequences. The seventh reaction offers a bright spot of connection, affirmation, and safety.

Empathize

We see suffering and are moved to action. We draw close with curiosity and care. We meet people where they are, not where we want them to be. We mourn when it's appropriate to mourn and weep when it's appropriate to weep. We affirm the reality of the pain. We ask to learn and listen to understand. We help carry the burden. We allow ourselves to feel what others feel. We remain vulnerable, share our resources (time, talent, treasure, connections, and opportunities), and engage. We enter THE PIT for the betterment of our community and its people.

Sounds like: "You make sense."

"What do you need from me right now?"

"I am with you."

"We will get through this together."

Silence—sitting together and listening.

We choose this reaction because:

We are moved by compassion and a sense of morality to acknowledge the suffering of others. We see people worthy of dignity, kindness, and respect. We are willing to put in the extra effort, get vulnerable, and stay committed. We courageously enter THE PIT because we are connected to something greater than ourselves.

Consequences for those in pain:

People feel valued, significant, and seen rather than judged and condemned. Safety is offered through the affirmation of value and a showing of trustworthiness. A relationship is grown. Change and healing can begin to take place.

We won't always get it right. Temptation to stay out of THE PIT and avoid the discomfort of pain can be high. We will make mistakes. Our goal is not perfection but to get quicker at recognizing when we dance around THE PIT, so we can make the necessary adjustments to get in THE PIT and offer connection, affirmation, and safety for those in pain.

"Most people just want someone to listen... without judgment."

How were you raised to handle pain? The next time you see suffering, how will you respond? Will you be someone's bright spot?

For over twenty years, Jeff Koziatek worked in the entertainment industry. He produced award-winning films and national touring shows, owned a complete event management company, acted in film and television, and performed in more than 4,000 shows across the country.

Today, Jeff is CEO at Core Authenticity. He helps people get clear on what they want, what gets in the way, where they want to go, how to get there, and how to use the super power of "No." The result—more personal freedom, more professional success, and more time living a bold, core authentic life.

His services include inspirational keynotes, trainings, and one-on-one coaching. He is a national speaker, author of the best-selling book *Blueprint for Value: 52 Habits to Discover and Strengthen Your Personal Worth*, and certified life coach with The Values Conversation and the John Maxwell TEAM.

www.coreauthenticity.com
jeff@coreauthenticity.com
www.facebook.com/coreauthenticity/
www.linkedin.com/in/jeffkoziatek/
www.vimeo.com/coreauthenticity

BARBARA A. STEWART

Unsung Heroes

I have always been curious about the fascination people have with superheroes and wondered how they differ from heroes in modern times. My favorite superhero is Wonder Woman. I am not sure exactly why, so I decided to do some research.

What I found out was not a surprise to me, as her values and superpowers were exactly what inspired me and led me to believe in the heroes I honor today during our changing times.

Superheroes give people hope. Their strength of character and morality allows them to overcome negative experiences and do good in the world. By emulating their traits, we can cope with adversity, allowing us to find meaning in loss; we can discover our strengths and use them for good.

Throughout my life, I have encountered several modern-day heroes. They are found in many areas of our lives. They are people who are noted for courageous acts or nobility of character.

An Unsung Hero, on the other hand, is best defined as a person who has achieved great things or performed acts of bravery, courage, or self-sacrifice, yet is not celebrated or recognized. They find impactful ways of connecting others to important resources, useful opportunities, and one another—and not primarily for their own benefit.

In this chapter, I am choosing our country's small business owners as my Unsung Heroes, as I honor their stories of adversity through unexpected and dramatic change. The examples of how these people have faced and endured their challenges can provide all of us with hope, strength, and courage in our own lives. We can be inspired by their examples of not giving up when things around them seem to fall apart. We can learn from these small business owners as they unassumingly use superhero powers that most of them do not even realize they have. When we become aware of the paths these Unsung Heroes have taken, we may be able to endure or adjust our own journey of change.

Small businesses are always experiencing change. At times it is what they thrive on, as it keeps their creativity at the forefront. Recently, a very unexpected change came along and dramatically affected our small businesses. When a small business is labeled as "nonessential," their opportunities become stripped away and a domino effect begins to happen. Traditionally, small businesses are built from a basic idea or passion. They build on that concept, invest both emotionally and financially, and constantly attract and nurture clients. When a small business is required to shut down or cut back with no notice or projection of when they can reopen, many things begin to happen. Desperation, fear, uncertainty, depression, health risks, and financial ruin take the forefront.

The trick, which most small businesses are known for, is to turn it around despite all odds. Even those businesses that experience total loss have an entrepreneur at the stern calculating that next creative endeavor and determining how they can facilitate growth.

Throughout the challenges, a few small business owners have stood up and spoken out, using their own plight to give others hope, courage, and a reason to go on. Others were affected so fast and hard and lost so much that they became physically ill. As they shared their stories, the rest of us became encouraged. I am inspired by these small business owners as they balance the importance of staying open to provide for their families, employees, and communities, while still understanding the importance of protecting the health of our most vulnerable populations.

Small business owners fit perfectly in my category of Unsung Heroes. They need to have a voice and be able to tell their stories as those are how we help each other heal and gain strength. Small businesses are important parts of history, and their actions provide a positive example for generations to follow.

As I revisit the attributes of my favorite superhero, Wonder Woman, I see a lot of the same qualities in these Unsung Heroes. Courage and creativity are inborn and are invaluable in their strategy and key to their longevity as a business.

I am excited to share words that describe both my superhero, as well as honor my deserving Unsung Heroes.

To some of my favorite Unsung Heroes that touched my life, who reopened for sake of livelihood of their staff and family, followed safety guidelines as they consistently overcame their challenges based on principle, who through the love of their clients provided hope, who, despite cancellations of events, fine-tuned their skills, and who put helping others in need at the forefront, I thank you. They used their superpowers of *strength, agility, endurance, durability, magic,* and *stamina.* They displayed their superhero characteristics of *master tactician, strategist,* and *field commander,* while using *deep emotional understanding* and *increased empathy.* My Unsung Heroes and my superhero are one in the same. They give the rest of us Hope.

All these heroes show strength of character that allows them to do good in the world. They never accept a barrier as a reason to stop.

See if you can find these heroic qualities in yourself and can identify them in others. You see, the world always changes. Sometimes abruptly and most often not how we expect it to. The ability to rise above is natural, though sometimes we feel like we do not have the energy. Embracing hope is the human attribute that connects us.

Whether you are a modern-day hero or an Unsung Hero in someone's mind, remind yourself of the fantasy superheroes that have been created for us throughout history. They are presented with the best qualities that we can strive for, and they have used these abilities to overcome many obstacles.

We all have superhero qualities within us, even if we do not get to wear the cool costume. Have courage, be creative, believe in yourself, and find someone who can remind you that who you are and what you do really does make a difference.

To all my Unsung Heroes….thank you.

Barbara A. Stewart, author of *The Caregiver's Guidebook*, has been credited with educating caregivers across the country on navigating the healthcare system. As a certified wellness coach, Barbara is sought after for her proactive and integrated approach to overall wellness. She complements her experience with her therapeutic massage business and her twenty years as a hospital pharmacy specialist.

Barbara has directed her passion toward providing inspiration to both caregivers and small business owners who have had to endure stressful changes. Barbara's firsthand experiences have given her more insight to help those affected. She offers encouragement and hope through courage and creativity. Her advice is sincere and simple.

Barbara's participation in *Bright Spots* will strengthen each reader's faith to move forward. Her interviews and presentations are dedicated to the unsung heroes by giving them a voice and helping them remember that who they are really does make a difference.

imb2002@att.net

www.caregiversguidebook.com

www.facebook.com/groups/458935254669702 (*The Caregiver's Guidebook*)

www.instagram.com/caregiversguidebook

DIANE FINNESTEAD

Imagine the Possibilities

Imagine if you did not know how to read. It is difficult to fathom not having that life skill because you are reading this chapter right now. Maybe you grew up in a household that loved books, with parents with degrees and careers, who read for pleasure or to learn new skills. This was the fabric of my household, passed down for generations. My mother, a speech pathologist and fourth-generation educator, believed that being a reader created leaders and learners.

Every night of my childhood, Mom read to my sister and me. As we snuggled into her, we became transported to new places and adventures. She voiced the imaginary worlds and brought to life the Golden Books, Dr. Suess, Shel Silverstein, and the *Little House on the Prairie* books. She sewed authentic costumes and added artifacts to our home, from butter churns to wagon wheels; the stories' settings became vacation destinations. Pure magic!

These experiences led me to enter the "family business" of education where I joined the fifth generation of educators. Then it snowballed, and I took on the challenge of promoting literacy.

The statistics are staggering and have been so for years. In 1995, researchers reported that, by the age of three, children showed a thirty-million-word gap[1]; today, the number may be closer to four million words. In 2002, thirty-two million adults could not read[2] and fifty percent of adults in the US could not read

---

1 Betty Hart and Todd R. Risely, "The Early Catastrophe: The 30 Million Word Gap by Age 3," *American Educator*, v27 n1 p4-9 Spr 2003.
2 Irwin S. Kirsch, Ann Jungeblut, Lynn Jenkins, and Andrew Kolstad, "Adult Literacy in America: A First Look at the Findings of the National Adult Literacy Survey," Adult Literacy in America. US Department of Education, Office of Educational Research and Improvement, April 2002, https://nces.ed.gov/pubs93/93275.pdf.

above the eight-grade level.[3] Ten years later, forty-three million US adults still possessed low English literacy skills.[4] Today, approximately two-thirds of America's children live in poverty with no reading materials of their own.[5] The disparity between higher socio-economic children and those living in poverty is significant, according to researcher Ruby Payne, PhD[6].

Bottom line, this is a gigantic divide in reading readiness.

As an educator, I was challenged to close this gap but didn't quite understand the problem until I came face to face with it. However, I was determined.

The first week as an elementary school principal, I rallied my troops and assembled a literacy team. We embarked on many projects to light and fuel the fire for reading.

One day, with the help of our library sponsor, we distributed enough books for every child to receive ten books at their reading level. We held an all-school summer reading contest, which had never been attempted in our school's history. It was the game-changer we had been looking for.

The kick-off was the last day of school. The names of 350-plus students were announced to music and under theatrical lighting in WrestleMania style. "Let's get ready to rumble!" It was fun, wild, free, and organized! To say the kiddos were excited is an understatement! Each student, some of whom had never owned a book before, received a new tote and ten of their chosen books. The buzz of excitement kept growing. When summer arrived, the halls were silent, and I wondered if the excitement would continue—would catch hold.

When the students returned in August, one fifth-grade boy corralled me. He burst out, "Principal Finnestead, I gotta put my total on the contest wall."

"How many books did you read?" I asked.

3 Valerie Strauss, "Hiding in Plain Sight," *The Washington Post*, November 1, 2016.
4 "43 Million American Adults Have 'Low' English Literacy Skills," *Language Magazine*, September 10, 2019, https://www.languagemagazine.com/2019/09/10/43-million-in-u-s-have-low-literacy-levels/.
5 Michelle Klampe and David Rothwell, "Nearly Two-Thirds of American Children Live in Asset Poverty, New Study Shows," February 20, 2019, https://today.oregonstate.edu/news/nearly-two-thirds-american-children-live-asset-poverty-new-study-shows.
6 Payne, Ruby, *Framework for Understanding Poverty*, 6th ed., 2018.

He smiled and said, "One hundred!" As I congratulated him, I asked how he read one hundred books if he only had ten. Grinning, he explained, "I read every book ten times!"

As it turns out, many students reported the same thing; some would recite excerpts from their books! Other compelling stories flooded in. Families became members of the library for the first time. Lives were transformed. It was no surprise that our school's reading scores soared after our summer reading contest initiative. This collective effort changed the trajectory for an entire school.

The gift of reading has endless benefits. Imagine the possibilities. Imagine the benefits of increased literacy; imagine better communication, greater understanding amongst all people regardless of class, not to mention the gains in educational opportunities, jobs, careers, relationships, choices, options, freedom, imagination, creativity, confidence, self-reliance, positivity, expression, appreciation; imagine higher employment, safer communities, and leadership, both personally and professionally.

Now, that is receiving the gift of reading!

You do not need a grandiose gesture to make a difference. You just need a gesture, and together we can make the gap decrease, one gesture at a time. Give the gift of reading so you can make a difference in your life, in the lives of those you love, and in your community.

Reading makes it possible and you make a difference.

Now, let's begin the possibilities.

Diane Finnestead has been a recognized leader in the field of life, health, and long-term-care insurance for the past twenty years. What sets Diane apart from other brokers is her ability to explain insurance options and communicate solutions with compassion and understanding to people of any age. This is the foundation that has built her award-winning insurance business. Diane is thankful for referrals and humbled to help thousands of Americans find the insurance coverage that is right for them.

Diane credits her ability to help so many due to her background and career in education. She holds a bachelor's degree in music from the University of North Texas, a master's in teaching, and an additional master's degree as an education specialist from Webster University. She also completed post-graduate work in music and education at the University of Memphis and Northwestern University.

www.dianeinsurancestl.com

https://www.linkedin.com/in/diane-finnestead-mat-ed-s-4187912a/

https://www.facebook.com/dianeinsurancestl

Diane Finnestead's literacy resources to imagine the possibilities

Ten awesome book charities that help kids all over the world: www.huffpost.com

Twenty places to donate used books: www.becomingminimalest.com

Where to donate used books; ten places to start: www.moneycrashers.com

Charities that give books and promote literacy: www.whatdowedoallday.com

Book donation programs, seeking book donations: https://libguides.ala.org/book-donations

Kids book club, subscription box ages zero to ten: www.bookroo.com

Books for kids/united states/ literacy non-profit: www.booksforkids.org

Where to donate books when you clean out your shelves: www.epicreads.com

Launching young readers: www.readingrockets.org

How to teach kids to read at home, ten simple steps: www.readingeggs.com

www.littlefreelibrary.org

www.scholastic.com

www.booksource.com

www.worldliteracyfoundation.org

www.adoptaclassroom.org

www.literacytrust.org.uk

www.familieslearning.org

www.worldreader.org

www.roomtoread.org

www.barbarabush.org

www.rif.org

www.reachoutandread.org

And many more. You are just a google search away from locating the possibilities in your community!

JUDITH GRIFFIN

Welcome to Butterfly Chats

What started out to be the worst year of my life, 2020, might end up being one of my most productive years. When the quarantine hit, followed by George Floyd's death, I said to myself that this was NOT going to beat me this time. You see, the 2008 recession paralyzed me. I was like a deer in headlights. I didn't know what to do. I looked to economists and others to tell me how it would end. While I was looking for answers, others pivoted and took control of their lives. When the recession was over, they had won. They reengineered their businesses, themselves; they created new lives.

My hometown of St. Louis, Missouri, is kind of a weird town in that we are beholden to our high schools. So, if you come to St. Louis be prepared for someone to ask you what school you went to; just know they're talking about your high school.

Some high school friends and I have remained friends. We get together about two to three times a year. It just so happened that the *challenges of 2020* hit around the time we were to get together. So, I suggested we do a Zoom party. I invited friends from the classes of '74, '75, and '76, and they invited classmates. We were all looking forward to it. That was in March.

The first thirty minutes of the first session was a comedy of errors, wrought with technology issues. The second session, we overcame the technology problems quickly, got into the Zoom meeting room, and had a good time getting caught up. People were enjoying themselves; then there as a lull in the conversation. That's when I decided to implement a new concept.

About five years ago, I had created a concept called "Butterfly Chats" to share information—educational or lifestyle information—with women. It was to serve

147

curious, like-minded women fifty years old or older, i.e., more mature women who can appreciate a certain lifestyle. But I knew I had to have a special way of introducing the concept. When the pandemic hit, Zoom was it. I invited friends from high school and others. From there, it grew to people from several countries joining in.

Every week we meet up at the same place, at the same time, for "girl talk." Participants show up in their most comfortable attire, sit in their favorite chair or couch, and grab the beverage of their choice. Butterfly Chats provides one hour per week when you can escape the news; it is not allowed. Whether an introvert or an extrovert, we can be ourselves at Butterfly Chats. All races, cultures—everyone feels welcome.

Butterfly Chats Happy Hours are a weekly destination for women on Thursday nights for an hour of "community chats." The Chats focus on a wide range of subjects, including travel, food, home, beauty, lifestyle, and culture, with self-care services being the larger portion of the focus; a virtual magazine.

Because of the level of maturity of the women I invite, I am very selective about the speakers. For example, when hiring a chef to do the cooking presentation, I was very clear that these women have been cooking all their lives, for families, children, and/or themselves. They are now at a stage in their lives where they don't want or don't like to cook. So, we needed items that could be prepared in fifteen minutes but would be impressive if we had to take them to a potluck event.

Just like any happy hour, we had presentations by spirit companies and a mixologist who demonstrated how to make alcoholic and nonalcoholic beverages and conversation. Mixologists were furloughed at the time, so we tipped them like we would at any happy hour. This was a way for us to support those that were directly affected by the quarantine.

We had makeup classes and haircare-while-quarantined classes; we learned about small businesses and not-for-profits; we had a chef and a hydroponic gardening presentation, wine pairings, wine tastings; we danced the night away with a DJ who played music from the eighties. We exercised with dancing classes and personal trainers. We even had after-parties. They were a blast! Some lasted as long as forty minutes after the program.

After being quarantined, haircare became a big issue for women. An African-American stylist talked about the simple things women could do to care for their hair while they were quarantined.

I loved putting the sessions together and the women seemed to love attending. Planning Butterfly Chats limited my time for watching the news and gave me pleasure bringing an hour of happiness to others. It was much needed at a time like this for the ladies and for me. A day or two after the session, I would email any recipes or product tips that were shared during the chat.

Today, Butterfly Chats' mission is to bring joy into the lives of the women in the midst of uncertainty. To provide an experience which allows females, fifty-plus years old, to gain new skills, knowledge, and/or learn about organizations that enhance their lifestyles in a fun, relaxed setting. We are growing and are preparing for season two which starts in October and will emphasize wine and other lifestyle topics.

There is something to be said for my high school friends. I don't know if I would have introduced Butterfly Chats or not if it had not been for them. They were my support system to get it off the ground, and I will always be grateful to them for that. I feel like this is my contribution to society and I won't sit back this time.

Judith "Judi" Griffin's passion for helping others drew her to the financial services industry in 2001. With a drive for advising and educating clients on how to achieve financial security, Judi eventually grew unsatisfied with how many firms prioritized production and quotas over clients' best interests and decided to strike out on her own. She founded Griffin Financial Services Group in St. Louis, Missouri, in 2010, and has expanded to include a team of advisors with locations in Atlanta, Georgia, and Pittsburgh, Pennsylvania.

Judi is a licensed Chartered Retirement Planning Counselor (CRPC®), Accredited Asset Management Specialist (AAMS®), and a two-time recipient of the Five Star Wealth Manager Award. She received her BA in business admin-istration from Clark Atlanta University and a master's in international business from Saint Louis University. She formerly served as an adjunct instructor at Wash-ington University in St. Louis. She is a frequent speaker on investment topics.

Judith@GriffinFinancials.com
www.GriffinFinancials.com

Join Butterfly Chats on Facebook and Instagram:
www.facebook.com/butterflychats
www.instagram.com/butterflychats/?hl=en

KRISTY BARTON

Sunshine

When I was a little girl, my nickname was "Merry Sunshine." It was perfect. The name encompassed my sunny disposition and almost-white blonde braids—I could have been the Swiss Miss Hot Cocoa twin. And even though I'm a tad bit older than my Swiss Miss look-alike, I have always tried to remain Merry Sunshine.

When the 2020 pandemic first hit—I'm not going to lie—I was pretty scared. I think my fear may have been a bit stronger than it would have been a couple of years ago. Now, I'm a mommy; and I not only have to keep myself safe, but I also have to worry about my son and husband. While fears of my personal life continued to rise in the past months, I also had to throw in the thought of what's going to happen to my business.

I started my public relations (PR)/marketing business, Sunshine Multimedia Consultants, almost six years ago. When I started, I had two goals for my business: work from home when I could and help the small business owner with all PR/marketing needs. Who knew that my forward-thinking, helpful mindset would pay off during a pandemic?

In the early months of 2020, work was pretty busy. And then the pandemic shutdown hit and my work went crazy busy.

I discovered that my little company could help more people than just in Missouri. By May 2020, I was helping clients in all four time zones. My workload on some days meant I could be on the phone for close to ten hours. The money and work were great. But I had a few meltdowns along the way because I was working so much and not traveling anywhere.

By now, I'm sure you've heard the word "pivot"; that is, when a business adapts—for example, to the pandemic—by making changes. Let's say a pizza joint adds services, expanded outdoor seating, or carry-out or frozen offerings so their most loyal customers don't have to go without their favorite pie. Those companies who learn to pivot often not only remain in business, but thrive. Several of my new clients have pivoted by starting new businesses during the height of the pandemic. You might think that idea seems a bit crazy, but those companies saw a need and now their new businesses are holding their own.

I've always loved to share my clients' businesses with a mass audience. During this "new normal," I have been able to not only share my clients' brands with millions of viewers, but along the way, my clients have also gone out of their way to give back to the communities that support them.

In case you didn't already know, TV is a great avenue to share brands. Some people might think it's easy to get on TV. Well, those people would be wrong. I have been in the PR/marketing business for more than 25 years. Let me just say that my journalism degree has been put to good use.

Now that I have clients in four different time zones, I'm on the phone and my laptop at all times of the day and wee hours of the morning. You see, when a client wants to be part of a TV segment on a morning show, discussions with the producer of said show may start around midnight. Some producers don't mind if you catch them at the beginning of their shift in those wee hours; most producers won't talk to you, though, until their morning show has ended. You could say it's like a cat-and-mouse kind of game. I'm pretty good at it. I'm always sunny even in the wee hours.

One of the things I love about getting my clients on TV is that they don't have to travel to the studio for the interview. The interview is done via Zoom or Skype. I have had clients in New York do interviews in Missouri and California. Today, thanks to technology, these coast-to-coast interviews can be done on the same day. The other advantage of being on TV is that stations will not only accept potential questions for said interview, but now, also, accept photos and videos to be used during the feature.

One of my biggest TV interview pet peeves is when someone on TV is wearing ear buds with a distracting dangling cord. The interviewee may also forget to elevate the computer screen, so the interview is done while looking up their nose. When I work with a client, I make sure they are well rehearsed for their TV interview. We go over lighting, what to wear, what kind of background to have—even ear buds.

I think we have all seen a whole lot happen in 2020. I started my company because I wanted to not only help people, but I also wanted flexibility to be with our child. My son, Jack, will turn two years old at the end of this year. To me, he's the perfect age. He has no clue what is going on. He doesn't even know he's missing anything throughout the quarantine since he's so young. We have kept him very isolated.

Our new normal has taught me a whole lot of things. First, you know who your friends are and who you should associate yourself with. I have always prayed for forgiveness and have been thankful for my blessings. I have also discovered that the more I help people, the more blessings I will get.

My nickname may be Merry Sunshine, but my life has not been easy. I have had to fight and struggle for everything I have in life. That fighter in me has become not only an ally to many, but even a force to be reckoned with in the pandemic. Some may say that my bright spot only appeared in 2020. I say it's been here all along, but now my shine is very bright.

Kristy Barton was born in southern Wisconsin and raised there until moving to Cheyenne, Wyoming, during middle school.

Throughout high school and college, Kristy managed the public relations (PR)/marketing needs for the Parks and Recreations Swim Department in Cheyenne. After college, Kristy freelanced for a bit until she was named Director of PR for a local union organization in St. Louis, Missouri. As the PR director for 18 years, Kristy developed and maintained a monthly magazine; negotiated, purchased, and created advertising; trademarked slogans, and helped raise hundreds of thousands of dollars for numerous charities and organizations.

In January 2015, Kristy started Sunshine Multimedia Consultants—a full-service PR/marketing firm. In this role, she has won numerous awards including the Webster Groves/Shrewsbury/Rock Hill Area Chamber of Commerce "Outstanding New Chamber Member" and back-to-back "Top 20 Best PR Firms in St. Louis" awards from the *St. Louis Small Business Monthly*.

Kristy earned her bachelor's degree in broadcast journalism from University of Missouri (Mizzou).

Kristy, her husband, Doug, and their son, Jack, reside in St. Louis, Missouri.

314-220-5050
Kristy@sunshinemultimediallc.com
Sunshinemultimediallc.com
www.facebook.com/Sunshine-Multimedia-Consultants-LLC

As we continue this pause, we encourage you to look for, and continue to create, your very own Bright Spots.

Right now, the world needs us to…

**Be Nice
Be Kind
Be Safe
Take Care
of Each Other
SHINE**

If you, or someone you know, would like to submit a chapter in one of our upcoming compilation anthologies, please visit daviscreative.com/anthology-services

Made in the USA
Columbia, SC
12 October 2020

22645111R00095